Books by Kenneth E. Long

Austrians vs. Keynesians -
The Great Debate

Economic Essentials - Theory and Application

Trump's Economic Era

Personal Finance -
Beware of Wolves in Sheep's Clothing

Introduction to Economics

AND THEY WILL RIOT
IN THE STREETS
A Nation Deceived
is a Nation Enslaved

by Kenneth E. Long

Rose of Sharon Publishers

Rose of Sharon Publishers
RoseofSharonPublishers@gmail.com

Cover design by
ArtTower / Pixabay - Brigitte Werner

ISBN13: 978-0-9963327-4-3 (print)
ISBN 13: 978-0-9963327-5-0 (ebook)

"You will own nothing and you will be happy"
—Klaus Schwab, World Economic Forum

"There is one thing in the world more wicked than the desire to command - and that is the will to obey."
—William Kingdom Clifford

Economist Norm Franz once stated:

"Gold is the money of kings, silver is the money of gentlemen, barter is the money of peasants — but debt is the money of slaves."

INTRODUCTION

There was a time when a country identified itself by ancestry and common ethnic nationality. Not so for America. If America abandons its political and economic structures, it will lose its identity more thoroughly than a country defined by a common ethnic and cultural background. America's identity is the institutions of personal liberty, free contracts, jury trials, uncensored news media, regular and free elections, open competition, private property rights, religious freedom, and habeas corpus. Fire and blood will come when citizens abandon these pillars of freedom.

CONTENTS

CHAPTER 1

CRIMES AGAINST HUMANITY

*T*he term Black Swan originates from the belief that there are only white swans. That opinion changed after a Dutch explorer discovered black swans in Australia. People consider low probability but high impact occurrences as black swan events. The black swan events of 911, the threat of global warming, and COVID-19 coupled with the Hegelian Dialectic method of control, advance a pre-determined agenda, such as revolutions, wars, lockdowns, vaccinations, and a one-world order.

The 19th-century German philosopher Georg Wilhelm Friedrich Hegel explained how an evil force could enslave humanity by entrapping us into a frenzied thought process leading to our destruction. By controlling the mainline news, social media, politics, education, and the voting process, this diabolical force has convinced societies to defend themselves against a false or at least an exaggerated threat. As long as society is ignorant of this invisible cabal of conspirators—freedom is threatened.

These puppet masters change cultures to fit their narrative by proposing a solution to a self-imposed problem. They instigate an event, watch for society's reaction, and formulate a solution (problem, response, resolution) that ushers in a foreordained consequence. However, the problem is always a red herring. A red herring event leads people to predetermined conclusions by constructing a false narrative. A red herring misleads people as a consequence of a black swan event. Nine-eleven, the threat of global warming, and COVID-19 are black swan events. The red herrings are the war on terror, strict environmental policies, and lockdowns. The Twin Towers attack ushered in the war on terror; the threat of global warming threatens our free enterprise system, and COVID-19 ushered in the fight against freedom. COVID-19 is the problem, the reaction is panic, and the consequence is the concentration of power.

COVID-19

According to the *New York Times*, COVID-19 policies are responsible for as many jobs lost as in the 1930s Great Depression and the 2008 Great Recession combined. Government programs, isolation at home, and the internet make unemployment less visible. The collateral damage resulting from the draconian lockdowns far outweigh the benefits.

WebMD gives its definition of the coronavirus: "*COVID-19 is a respiratory condition caused by a coronavirus. Some people are infected but don't notice any symptoms. Most people will have mild symptoms and get better on their own. But about 1 in 6 will have severe problems, such as trouble breathing. The odds of more serious symptoms are higher if you're older or have another health condition like diabetes or heart disease.*"

When the Frontline Doctors gave their press conference on the Supreme Court's steps, they admonished us not to be afraid of COVID-19. On their website, they write: "*We exist to counter the massive disinformation campaign regarding the pandemic. We are diverse, exceedingly well-credentialed physicians with extensive front line experience treating both COVID-19 and the dangerous health effects due to the lockdowns. There are many early treatment options! Most people do just fine!*" The doctors claim that hydroxychloroquine

(HCQ)is an effective drug for the virus, but the US and Canada have banned it.

In her book, *I Do Not Consent: My Fight Against Medical Cancel Culture*, Doctor Simone Gold states that Hydroxychloroquine (HCQ) is safe and effective against COVID-19. It was only subject to a shifting consensus in the days and weeks after Donald Trump publicly acknowledged its use as an effective treatment. All of a sudden, HCQ was regarded as a dangerous snake oil even though doctors worldwide routinely prescribe it.

Despite the success of HCQ, the Center for Disease Control (CDC) announced that there were no approved drugs to treat COVID-19. Dr. Gold states, *"The prohibition against HCQ contradicted everything I had learned about medicine since I worked as a young intern. Before 2020, every doctor all over the world knew HCQ was safe."* Soon many state governors ordered doctors not to prescribe HCQ and the World Health Organization reinforced the anti-HCQ narrative. Dr. Gold believes we can manage the virus carefully and intelligently, but we cannot live with fear. Because Dr. Gold dared confront the establishment, she was censored by social media, terminated from her job, and viciously attacked in the press, all for prescribing what she believed was the best treatment for her patients.

COVID Operation: What Happened, Why It Happened, and What's Next is a book by Pamela A. Popper and Shane D. Prier. The book explains the COVID-19 hoax, the major players in the deception, and the events. It reveals how easily people can lose their dignity, personhood, and freedom without holding the government, world leaders, or the news media accountable. The culprits have waged war against humanity while disguising themselves as public servants, health professionals, and other do-gooders.

Corona Investigative Committee

Reiner Fuellmich is a lawyer in Germany and California specializing in fraudulent corporations. He is one of four members of the German Corona Investigative Committee. The committee believes a class action lawsuit is necessary against individuals and institutions who have exaggerated and spread lies about COVID-19. The committee is concerned with how dangerous the virus is and the significance of a positive PCR test. Doctors administer Polymerase Chain Reaction (PCR) tests to detect genetic material from a specific organism, such as a virus. Dr. Fuellmich states:

> *"I will now explain to you how and where an international network of lawyers will argue this biggest tort case ever, the corona fraud scandal, which has meanwhile unfolded into probably the greatest crime against humanity ever committed."*

The committee will prove that whatever is causing the symptoms attributed to COVID-19 causes no more hospitalization or death than the seasonal flu. The PCR test is incapable of detecting COVID-19. The sole purpose of PCR testing is to generate large numbers of false-positive results called "cases" and frighten the population into passively accepting vaccines and restructuring society without question.

Previously a pandemic was considered a disease that spread worldwide, leading to severe illnesses and deaths. In 2008, the World Health Organization (WHO) dropped the requirements of diseases and deaths. This new definition enabled WHO to declare the swine flu in 2009 and COVID-19 as pandemics. Because of one person's opinion, Christian Heinrich Maria Drosten, a German virologist, in March of 2020, the German Bundestag announced the COVID-19 an epidemic and ordered a lockdown and the suspension of constitutional rights with no legal basis, without doing a cost-benefit analysis, and without seeking contrary opinions. When the German lawyer, Beate Bahner, a specialist in medical law, criticized Berlin's coronavirus policies, the authorities had her committed to a psychiatric institution. When a French music producer left his studio without a mask, three policemen pounced on him and beat him with a truncheon for five minutes. The pandemic has militarized events and mirror the post-1929 Weimar Republic, and the new Brownshirts are officials who terrorize citizens for not wearing masks and not cooperating with lockdown rules.

PCR tests are essential because they became the justification for worldwide lockdowns, social distancing, and mandatory face masks. According to Dr. Fuellmich, these tests are useless for detecting infections, and the inventor of the PCR test, Dr. Kary B. Mullis, claims that the test does not detect infectious disease. Dr. Mullis died unexpectedly in August of 2019. When four Germans were quarantined in Portugal after authorities judged one of them positive for COVID-19, a court in a 34-page ruling included the following: Given current scientific evidence, this test shows itself to be unable to determine beyond a reasonable doubt that such positivity corresponds, in fact, to the infection of a person by the COVID-19 virus.

John Pombe Joseph Magufuli

John Pombe Joseph Magufuli was the fifth president of Tanzania, serving from 2015 until his death in March 2021. He was suspicious of World Health Organization policies and set out to prove its falsehood concerning the coronavirus. So he sent samples of animals, fruit and motor oil, most of them came back positive for the virus.

> *"We took samples from goats and sheep. We sent samples from car oil ... And we even named all the samples. Like the sample of car oil we named Jabil Hamza, 30 years old, male. We took samples from (a bird) we named Kware. The results came back positive for Covid-19."*

Health care systems were never in danger of becoming overwhelmed because the mortality rate of Covid is equal to the seasonal flu. Even the United States Center for Disease Control and Prevention (CDC) agrees PCR tests are not reliable and can lead to false conclusions. Elon Musk, the billionaire and founder of Tesla, had four PCR tests done on the same day, in the same place, and by the same nurse; two results came back positive, and two were negative. Several highly respected scientists believe that there has never been a Corona pandemic, only a PCR-test scam. Dr. Mike Yeadon is a former Vice-President and Chief Science Officer at Pfizer. He and other well-known scientists published a scientific paper in September of 2020 in which they wrote:

> *"We're basing our government policy, our economic policy, and the policy of restricting fundamental rights, presumably on completely wrong data and assumptions about the coronavirus ... We have explained how a hopelessly performing diagnostic test has been, not for diagnosis of disease, but it seems solely to create fear."*

The so-called "Panic Paper," written by the German Department of the Interior, reveals that the population was deliberately driven to panic by politicians and the mainstream media without justification. Naysayers do not dispute that Covid-19 is dangerous, but records have shown that most deaths have been older adults with pre-existing conditions. Germany became the center of massive lobbying by the pharmaceutical and tech industry because the world should do as the Germans do to survive the pandemic.

It is apparent to all who are paying attention that the COVID-19 scandal is a deliberate attack on democracy, which is in danger of being replaced by fascist totalitarian models. In Australia, police arrest people who do not wear masks or wear them incorrectly. In the Philippines, they run the risk of getting shot in the head. In other countries, authorities take children away from their parents if they do not comply with quarantine regulations. Los Angeles forces nursing home patients and indigent people to be vaccinated. Coronavirus policies traumatize people, especially children, cause respiratory problems, and will usher in a depression. Irrational behavior has replaced common sense because mandates are not about protection. They are about control.

Doctor Scott Atlas, physician, a scholar of public health, member of the Hoover Institution, and former health advisor to President Donald Trump, gives talks on the efficacy of lockdowns, social distancing, and closings. According to Dr. Atlas, if we do a cost-benefit analysis of the lockdown, we get a bleak picture indeed—the costs have far outweighed the benefits. When the government banned all non-essential procedures, doctors did not do thousands of biopsies of potential cancers, doctors did not perform knee and hip replacements or do biopsies of possible cancers or schedule cancer screenings. People who may have made appointments before the virus for ailments went untreated for fear of going to the doctor's office, and others with strokes failed to call for an ambulance, and children did not get their vaccinations. Consequently, hospitals have lost millions of dollars due to Covid policies.

Thousands of despair deaths happen when people lose their jobs and businesses, face wage cuts, or go bankrupt. Virus policies have caused more lost years of life than would have been the case in a no-policy world. Since Dr. Atlas made remarks questioning the effectiveness of masks, Twitter removed his tweets, claiming that his comments had misleading information and violated the COVID-19 agenda. Atlas told *Newsweek* he had appealed the decision, adding: Twitter seems to be censoring the science if it goes against their own goals of public indoctrination. *Forbes Magazine* has called Dr. Atlas an evil scientist for not deferring to the official narrative, not adhering to the prevailing orthodoxy.

Doctor Atlas recommends opening all schools because school-age children are not susceptible to the virus, and they need structure and physical contact with their friends. There are virtually zero risks of death and almost zero risks of a severe illness in children. Of the first hundred-plus-thousand deaths analyzed, 99.98 deaths were not in children, and there is practically no chance of children transmitting the disease to their parents or teachers; it is irrational to close the schools. Online learning cannot replace the quality of in-person instruction even in the best-case scenario, especially when at least half of students are not logging into their lessons. Emergency room doctors are reporting an increase in severe child abuse cases and drug overdoses by adults. Many people making $40,000 a year or less have lost their jobs due to COVID-19 restrictions.

CLASS ACTION LAW SUIT

Thorsten Schleif, a former president of the federal constitutional court in Germany, claims, *"German citizens are currently experiencing the most severe encroachment on their constitutional rights since the founding of the federal republic of Germany in 1949."* Based on criminal law rules, asserting false facts concerning the PCR tests, or intentional misrepresentation, we can only assess fraud. The German professor of civil law, Martin Schwab, supports this finding in public interviews. He has provided a detailed account of the mainstream media's complete failure to report on the facts of this so-called pandemic. World governments have applied rules for social distancing, mandatory mask-wearing, and public places closures based on false facts, half-truths, and exaggeration.

Under the civil tort law rules, all those harmed by PCR-test-induced lockdowns should receive total compensation, and leaders should label virus policies as a crime against humanity. According to legal experts, a class action lawsuit may be the only way to bring this madness to an end. A judge can allow a class-action case to go forward if questions revolve around the worldwide PCR-test-based lockdowns and their consequences.

German tort lawyers started a lawsuit against the World Health Organization (WHO), and they expect American and Canadian lawyers to follow suit. Belgian health experts are demanding a full investigation into the WHO for the pandemic. Russia's national health watchdog claims that shutting down the economy to prevent the coronavirus spread is pointless and makes no sense. Tort lawyers have received expert opinions proofing that PCR tests cannot detect infections. An anti-vaccination group is suing Canadian Prime Minister Justin Trudeau for $11 million over his coronavirus response. Mont-St-Hilaire lawyer Jean-Felix Racicot filed a challenge in Saint-Hyacinthe court in 2020, arguing that Quebec's laws enacted to halt the spread of COVID-19 should be null and void.

GREAT RESET

The *World Economic Forum* (https://www.weforum.org) and the book *Covid-19: The Great Reset* by Klaus Schwab and Thierry Malleret assure us that the modern world after the pandemic will be better, more inclusive, more equitable, and more respectful of Mother

Nature once we reset the present social/economic system and replace it with a new and better one. There is no hidden agenda. When the elitists get together and talk about their plans for the future, all we have to do is listen to them because they tell us where the world is heading. *You will own nothing and you will be happy.*

In chapter 2, the authors show us how past epidemics have altered society and how COVID-19 can do the same today. They write in detail about how germ phobia will reshape society. Chapter 4 calls for a restructuring of the world's economy and a global government. In their conclusion, on page 243, they ask the question: *Could Covid-19 have the force to ignite profound changes?*

According to the *Forum*, Covid-19 will usher in the Great Reset. The puppet masters seek to put us in bondage and debt by eliminating private property, phasing out the free enterprise system, installing fake democracy, controlling the media, and replacing Judeo-Christian western values with paganism. The purpose of the bankruptcies, unemployment, and government debt increase is to put us in bondage.

Johns Hopkins University had a report published in 2017 titled The Spars Pandemic 2025-2028. This 89-page report discusses a fictional pandemic where Big Pharma orchestrates global domination. The authors write as if someone in 2030 is looking back on a pandemic that swept the world between 2025 and 2028. The report advocates that governments must impose control over their citizenry by cooperating in a global governing body. This charade only works if enough people voluntarily cooperate with the puppet masters.

Event 201 is a 2019 paper published by the Bill and Melinda Gates Foundation, Johns Hopkins Center for Health Security, and the World Economic Forum. Event 201 simulated how the world would respond to a fictional world coronavirus pandemic known as CAPS. The paper predicted that 65 million people would die, that there would be massive lockdowns, quarantines, censorship of alternative viewpoints under the guise of fighting "disinformation," and suggested arresting people who question the pandemic narrative.

The Great Reset is the fulfillment of George Orwell's novel *1984*, where authorities monitor Oceania's citizens and issue fabricated news stories that adhere to the party line. If you remove the historical records you remove the history. Authorities convince citizens to worship a mythical government leader called Big Brother, while it gives nonsense statements like "WAR IS PEACE, SLAVERY IS FREEDOM, IGNORANCE IS STRENGTH." In this Orwellian world, power is centralized, and the establishment punishes anyone who speaks or acts against its tyranny. George Orwell saw the future when he wrote, *"History has stopped. Nothing exists except an endless present in which the Party is always right."*

The puppet masters use public safety as an excuse, and tyranny results from anti-freedom laws. As long as we demand protection from real or perceived threats, authorities can oblige us only by eliminating free speech, competition, entrepreneurship, innovation, freedom of expression, and the Christian church. The Christian church is a target because it teaches that we cannot serve God and mammon. Unchecked power in the hands of a few always leads to tyranny.

The Great Reset is a coordinated plan that has been years in the making before the virus. It is a social and economic world transformation that will centralize power in fewer hands through Orwellian surveillance technologies. Yuval Noah Harari wrote an article for the Financial Times titled "The World After the Coronavirus." The opening sentence reads:

"This storm will pass. But the choices we make now could change our lives for years to come. Technology has made it possible for the

government to monitor and punish anyone who dare break the rules."

The City of London Corporation, in collaboration with the *Green Finance Institute* and supported by the *World Economic Forum*, hosted a virtual summit that focused on the role of green finance in the Great Reset. Attendees discussed putting the frameworks into place and funnel finance into a net-zero carbon emissions economy, shutting down carbon-producing industries, and reducing the world's population. This conference's critical element discussed how the world would transition from our current system to a green new deal.

While Amazon does not censor Schwab/Malleret's book and others that support the prevailing agenda, it does remove books contrary to the globalist agenda. After James Perloff sold 3,500 copies of his book *Covid-19 and the Agendas to Come: Red-pilled*, Amazon banned the book from its website, claiming: *"We reserve the right to determine whether content provides a poor customer experience and remove the content from sale."* You can find a list of books Amazon banned on the internet.

AGENDA 21 and AGENDA 2030

Agenda 21 (1992) offers a detailed plan for "Sustainable Development" that countries should implement. Building upon Agenda 21, world leaders met in New York City in 2015 to present a new fifteen-year plan entitled "Transforming Our World: the 2030 Agenda for Sustainable Development." The difference between Agenda 21 and Agenda 2030 is that Agenda 2030 encompasses more than the environment; it calls for governments seizing control of the means of production. This is communism.

Instead of traditional capitalism, the group stated that the world should adopt more socialistic policies, such as wealth taxes, additional regulations, and massive Green New Deal government programs. The Green New Deal is a congressional resolution that lays out a grand plan for tackling climate change The purpose of the Great Reset is a complete overhaul of the world's existing structures and institutions.

NINE-ELEVEN

Before September 1, 2001, terrorism had been considered a criminal offense, not an act of war. As a criminal offense, the Constitution stipulates procedural rights and guarantees that protect citizens from an overzealous government. The basic idea is to allow people to respond to the accusations within a judicial process. However, the Bush Administration declared the attack on the Twin Towers an act of war, negating the judicial process and opening the door to invade Iraq and other countries without the chance of rebuttal.

On September 13, 2001, only two days after the attack, Congress passed the Authorization for the Use of Military Force (AUMF) Act, which gives the President the authority to: *"use all necessary and appropriate force against those nations, organizations, or persons he determines planned, authorized, committed, or aided the terrorist attacks that occurred on September 11, 2001."* On the same day, President George W. Bush signed the act into law, giving Congress the authority to fund the war on terror. In the first sixteen years, the government used AUMF to justify military operations in 14 countries. According to the census bureau, there are 3.3 million veterans who have served since September 11, 2001.

I have taken most of the following information about 911 from "Episode 308 - 9/11 Trillions: Follow the Money" of the Corbett Report. The Port Authority of New York and New Jersey agreed to privatize the World Trade Center in 1998. In April of 2001, Larry

Silverstein already owned World Trade Center Building 7, which collapsed into its footprint within minutes of the incident even though a plane never hit it. He signed a 99-year lease from the Port Authority of New York for $3.2 billion for the Twin Towers and Buildings 4 and 5. With only 4.0625% down, $14 million, Silverstein Properties was able to close the deal. As a prerequisite to finalizing the agreement, Silverstein insisted that insurance had to be double the previous coverage, from $1.5 billion to $3.55 billion. He also emphasized that the Silverstein Group had the explicit right to rebuild and expand the structures should they be destroyed.

Only six months later and within hours of the incident, Silverstein pressured his lawyers to claim separate insurable events instead of one. Silverstein spent years in the courts attempting to win $7.1 billion from his $3.55 billion insurance policy, and in 2007 he walked away with $4.55 billion, the largest single insurance settlement ever. Silverstein then sued United and American Airlines for a further $3.5 billion for negligence. Silverstein's profit comes to more than $7.5 billion! That is a 70-fold return—not bad for a 14-million-dollar investment!

President George W. Bush waited 441 days before appointing the 9-11 Commission, naming Dr. Henry Kissinger as chair. Kissinger's first appointment was with family members of 9-11 victims. When a family member asked him if he had any Saudi clients, he stalled, stammered, and resigned the next day. President Bush then appointed Thomas Cain and Lee Hamilton to co-chair the commission. During the process, both chairs and four other commissioners expressed concern that the authorities were misleading the group. Thomas Kean and Lee Hamilton wrote a book published in 2006 titled *Without Precedent: The Inside Story of the 9/11 Commission*. The book explores the coverup and explains how the political insiders set up the commission to fail. At one point, the commission considered bringing charges against Pentagon officials who had lied to them. Although the 9-11 whistleblowers have done everything possible to tell their story, they have been ignored, vilified, shunned by colleagues, smeared by the press, and fired from their jobs.

The American Institute of Architects for 9/11 Truth has more than 3,000 architects and engineers with over 25,000 years of experience and over 28,000 members who demand a new investigation. They all agree that a localized failure in a steel-framed building cannot cause a catastrophic collapse. Loose Change: An American Coup is a documentary revealing how 9-11 was an inside job.

GLOBAL WARMING

Greta Thunberg is a Swedish Joan of Arc for the climate movement as she leads children worldwide in a crusade to convince parents that they must fix the planet lest the world end before they are adults. The threat of global warming is an example of the Hegelian Dialectic in action: problem, reaction, solution. As a keynote speaker at the UN, she admonished members, *"We are at the beginning of mass extinction, yet all you can talk about is money. You are failing us."* The United Nations encourages all nations to limit their carbon footprint and follow the Paris Agreement on Climate Change to achieve its sustainable development goals. Young people all over the world are being terrified of an impending dark future.

Now meet Dr. Patrick Michaels, the director of the Center for the Study of Sciences and a senior fellow in environmental studies at the Cato Institute. His Ph.D. thesis was on climate change, and he is a past president of the American Association of State Climatologists and chairman of the American Meteorological Society. He was a research professor of environmental sciences at the University of Virginia for 30 years, an author and reviewer of the United Nations Intergovernmental Panel on Climate Change, and a recipient of the

Nobel Peace Prize in 2007. Dr. Michaels claims that government computer models make dramatic systematic errors. There are 32 families of computer models used by the United Nations, and they all predict too much global warming.

Now meet Ian Rutherford Pilmer, an Australian geologist, professor emeritus of earth sciences at the University of Melbourne, an active writer of scientific papers and six books. When not busy with his position as the director of the Center for the Study of Science at the Cato Institute, he talks about the hoax of global warming and the games politicians play to formulate policy. He emphasizes that the earth's temperature has always been in flux, and he explains how the belief in climate change has become a new kind of morality, a religion. A movie on the subject is *The Great Global Warming Swindle*, 2007. The documentary reveals that everything environmentalists have told us about global warming is untrue, and this falsehood is a threat to humanity.

Dr. Mototaka Nakamura has a Doctorate of Science from the Massachusetts Institute of Technology (MIT). He has spent his career in abnormal weather and climate change at MIT, Georgia Institute of Technology, NASA, Jet Propulsion Laboratory, California Institute of Technology, JAMSTEC, and Duke University. In his book, *The Global Warming Hypothesis is an Unproven Hypothesis*. He explains why generally accepted information about global warming is untrustworthy.

So why does the Environmental Protection Agency (EPA) accuse carbon dioxide of global warming? Because the Supreme Court told the EPA in 2007 that if it found that carbon dioxide endangered human health and welfare, it had the power to regulate under the Clean Air Act. So the models had to implicate carbon dioxide to justify the EPA's authority. If people believe that global warming is a problem and only the government can solve the problem, they will support an ever-larger government as a trade-off with personal freedom.

Meanwhile, the news does not report on Dr. Art Robinson winning the Voice of Reason Award at the 9th International Conference on Climate Change. He received 31,000 signatures by the world's leading scientists, 9,000 of them with PhDs, on a document denying global warming as a problem. Dr. Robinson believes that the political left has hijacked the subject, and the news has ignored real scientists. Extreme environmentalists have three strings to their bow.

(1)They think that everyone agrees with them.

(2) It is unnecessary to discuss the science because they are on the right side of the debate.

(3) and that everyone who opposes them has a commercial self-interest.

Dr. Judith Curry is a professor and former Chair of the School of Earth and Atmospheric Sciences at the Georgia Institute of Technology. She delivered a speech to the US Senate Commerce Committee debunking global warming while claiming that environmental scientists have become groupthink victims. There is evidence that Dr. Curry is correct. The Intergovernmental Panel on Climate Change reported that the global surface temperature measured by weather satellites had shown a much smaller increasing linear trend over the past 15 years than over the past 30 to 60 years. This evidence has caused the Green Movement to claim that we are in a "pause" or a "global warming hiatus." A study conducted by a Finnish research team has found little evidence to support the idea of man-made climate change and that current climate models fail to take into account the effects of cloud coverage and sun cycles on global temperatures. Researchers in Japan corroborated the results of the investigation.

Lawlessness breeds intolerance, and once we go down this road, extremes become the norm. The Portland Public School board unanimously approved a resolution that bans textbooks and other teaching materials that deny climate change exists or cast doubt on whether humans are to blame. The rule also mandates a curriculum and educational opportunities that address climate change and climate justice in all Portland public schools. If the topic of global warming, or global change, was a purely economic issue, we could have a dialog among differing opinions. But the global warming movement has become a religion, a slow creep to further global domination.

THE LEGAL GUARDIAN CRIME

According to Robert Sarhan MD, the inheritance of Americans is being stolen from an insidious plot that no one is immune to becoming a victim. No law or legal system can protect us from this crime against humanity. When Dr. Sarhan pleaded before Circuit Judge D. Bruce Levy, a Miami-Dade probate judge, to appoint him as his mother's legal guardian, the judge brought an attorney into the case, and the attorney brought in scores of other professionals including around-the-clock nurses and maids.

Even though his mother was competent, citing discord between Sarhan and his brother, Circuit Judge D. Bruce Levy appointed a professional guardian over his mother's estate. In such instances, the court-appointed guardian has complete control over one's estate, including all finances. In some cases, authorities with a legal court order commit the victim to a carefully guarded nursing home where they are stripped of any means of communication and put on a heavy dose of mind-numbing medication. After the criminals drain the victims' estate, accomplices give the person a drug overdose, resulting in death.

Netflix has a movie about the situation titled *I Care a Lot*. The film stars Rosamund Pike and has garnered enough views to be one of Netflix's most popular movies. In the movie, Marla Grayson and her partner, Fran, bribe medical professionals to declare older people legally unfit to look after themselves and then convince a gullible judge into appointing her as the victim's guardian. The movie is fictional, but the storyline is real.

> *"Our parent's estates are being stolen and our parents are being murdered, by probate court judges, attorneys and guardians ... The United States has become a 'Lawless America' ... Top government officials, are destroying this country and stealing between 500 Billion to a trillion dollars per year from the American people."*
> —Dr. Robert Sarhan MD

CHAPTER 2

A NATION DECEIVED
IS A NATION ENSLAVED

*T*he difference between a Nationalist and a Globalist is the difference between paper and blood. Globalists are concerned with what is legal and official, like a document that legalizes citizenry. Nationalists care about genetics and heredity. I could migrate to Japan, become a legal citizen, and learn to speak Japanese, but I will never be Japanese because blood is stronger than paper.

Globalists want to centralize control in a world governing body. The United Nations Secretary-General Antonio Guterres has stated in typical Orwellian speak that no one wants a world government—but we must work together to improve world governance, while saying that the UN's goal is a one-world government by 2030. Globalists prefer a top-down solution to problems; nationalists prefer decentralization and a bottom-up approach. Globalists share ideals, such as cultural diversity, different gender identities, and gay marriage. Nationalists believe in individualism, where there is freedom of choice within a democratic republic. People still work together collectively under the rule of law, but their interaction is voluntary. Nationalists prefer secure borders; they are not against foreigners, but they demand that immigrants assimilate themselves into the country and respect the rule of law.

They wish to protect their nation regarding common birth, race, history, language, customs, and traditions.

Western civilization's identity lies in nationalism, the rule of law, freedom of speech, faith in God of the Bible, the separation of power, and freedom from oppression by claiming our rights come from God and not from man. Western civilization is rooted in Judeo-Christian beliefs—but Christians are being persecuted, especially in the Middle East, the cradle of Christianity, where adherents face extinction. Christianity has become politically incorrect in the West because Globalists see Christianity as an enemy of secularism. The press rarely depicts Christians as the underdogs, and therefore, it is politically incorrect to defend Christianity.

Christians began to lose their grip on America when six Supreme Court judges decided to remove prayer from public schools. When society takes God out of the equation, the state reigns supreme. Progressives believe that man is born good and that if people follow their true nature, there would be peace on earth; God is not recognized; therefore, they commit the sin of pride. Christians believe that sin is a part of human nature and that people can only achieve goodness when they know and obey God's tenants as put forth in the Bible. Globalists have a hatred for Christians because Christian beliefs conflict with the goal of a new world order. The masters of the universe have engraved the objectives of the New World Order on the Georgia Guidestones.

In a field seven miles north of Elberton on Georgia highway 77 stands the Georgia Guidestones, also known as the "American Stonehenge." The Guidestones is a massive granite 19-foot high monument that displays a 10-part message espousing the conservation of humanity and future generations in 12 languages. The names of four ancient languages are inscribed on the top: Babylonian cuneiform, Classical Greek, Sanskrit, and Egyptian Hieroglyphics. The twelve messages engraved on the stones deal with governance and establishing a world government, population and reproduction control, the environment and man's relationship with nature, and spirituality.

A group of white individuals of different ethnic groups with other languages is exophobic (tending to discriminate against various groups), homophobic (having negative attitudes against lesbian, gay, bisexual, and transgender people), anti-Semitic (against Jews), and racist. To be diverse, a group must represent more than one national origin, color, religion, socioeconomic group, and sexual orientation. Globalists bludgeon white cultures to show more compassion for disadvantaged groups of non-white and non-traditional people. How can one turn a blind eye to the suffering of others?

Betty, a freelance journalist, used to get a decent amount of assignments for female writers, but now every post says, "BIPOC writers only." BIPOC is an acronym for Black, Indigenous, and People of Color. Globalists believe that diversity can enhance livelihood, but it produces conflict and destroys social cohesion. Virginia has a law that compels churches, religious schools, and Christian ministries to hire employees who do not share their stated beliefs on marriage, sexuality, and gender identity. They must include in their health plans coverage for sex reassignment surgeries. These laws violate the Virginia Religious Freedom Restoration Act and provisions of the Virginia Constitution.

GENDER IDENTITY

While sex refers to biology, gender is about your sense of who you are as a human being. California became the first state to allow its residents to opt for a gender-neutral designation on birth certificates. You can choose your gender identity in New York City from a list of 31 politically correct genders, one for each day of the month! While Facebook has always used sex terms (male and female) to describe users' sex, it recognizes 51 gender options. Transgender need not be one sex to the opposite sex; transgender can be anything. Title IX is the federal law that protects us against gender-based discrimination; it states: "No person in the United States shall, based on sex, be excluded from participation in, be denied the benefits of, or be subjected to discrimination under any education program or activity receiving Federal financial assistance." Prisoners in California and Massachusetts can request where the state will incarcerate them based on whether they identify as male or female regardless of their birth sex.

The last generation of counterculture rebellion has become this generation of hate—we stand on the precipice of another cultural shift where the most radical elements forcefully impose their will on society by establishing a TechnnoFascist community by controlling our thoughts. There was Obergefell versus Hodges in 2015 when the Supreme Court ruled that the Constitution guarantees same-sex couples the right to marry. Then there was Bostock versus Clayton County in 2020. The Court held that Title VII of the Civil Rights Act of 1964 protects employees against discrimination because of their sexual orientation or gender identity. Colleges now have penalties for non-followers of their thought and speech codes.

People lose their jobs for refusing to address people by their preferred gender or have an opinion contrary to the official narrative. In Virginia, the Fairfax County School District removed the phrase "biological gender" from its curriculum and replaced it with the words "sex assigned at birth." The new legislation also makes it easier for individuals to change their gender on birth certificates. California and Oregon offer a gender-neutral option for a driver's license. It is illegal for healthcare professionals to "willfully and repeatedly" refuse to use a patient's preferred pronoun in California. In New York City, landlords and business owners who intentionally use the wrong pronoun with transgender workers and tenants face potential fines of as much as $250,000. Peter Vlaming, a high school teacher in

Virginia, was fired from his job when he used the wrong pronoun when speaking to another teacher about a transgender student. A man in British Columbia, Canada, was sent to prison for six months for not referring to his fourteen-year-old transgender daughter as he instead of she. Joshua Sutcliffe, an Oxfordshire teacher, was suspended when he said, "well-done girls." He misgendered a transgender student in a group.

This trend is growing even though the Supreme Court has ruled that compelled speech is not free speech. Dr. David Mackereth from Dudley, West Midlands, England, was terminated from his job when he told his manager that he would never call a six-foot-tall bearded man madam. When he brought the case before the employment tribunal, the tribunal ruled that his biblical beliefs have no place in British society.

The lesbian, gay, bisexual, transgender, and queer (LGBTQ) community preach tolerance, but they are intolerant to opposing viewpoints. When Päivi Räsänen quoted the Bible on Facebook condemning homosexuality, Romans 1:24-27, Finland's authorities charged her with incitement against sexual and gender minorities. Shortly after Chick-Fil-A opened its first restaurant in England, demonstrations against Chick-Fil-A's anti-LGBTQ views forced the restaurant chain to suspend operations.

The LGBTQ movement does not unite people; it divides us. For example, the United Methodist Church (UMC) has devised a plan whereby the UMC can expel all their conservative members who still adhere to the biblical teaching about homosexuality, as found in Matthew 19:4-6. So if you do not support the LGBTQ community, you may not be welcome as a UMC member. All the other mainline American churches had already gone pro-LGBTQ, and the UMC was the last bastion of resistance to changing mores. This belief goes beyond the premise that one can hate the sin but love the sinner.

MULTICULTURALISM

Multiculturalists discriminate against white, straight males and Christians while considering non-white heterosexuals, transgender people, women, Jews, and Muslim victims. The University of Michigan held a two-day seminar teaching employees how to deal with their "whiteness." The university spent $85 million to increase campus diversity and paid its chief diversity officer $385,000 per year. Some universities are concerned with outward appearance while suppressing a difference of opinion. The University of Vermont hosts retreats where it stresses that differences in outcomes are due to privileges granted to white males. Some universities require students to take courses in diversity as a requirement for graduation.

A student at Marquette University criticized an ethics professor for telling a student he could not criticize the practice of same-sex marriage in her class because that would be "homophobic." Multiculturalism does not allow criticism on issues that are offensive to a protected group. When another professor defended the student and refused to apologize for his defense, the university fired him.

Teaching the classics has become an anomaly on many college campuses. For example, Seattle University students held a week-long sit-in to protest the college's classical emphasis. The sit-in led to the dean's departure after a student complained about having to read works from "dead white people." Students at Oregon Reed College staged a protest claiming that too many courses were "caucasoid" and "eurocentric" and "oppressive." Yale's English Department changed its curriculum after 150 students signed a petition demanding a change. It is now possible to get an English degree from Yale without studying Chaucer, Shakespeare, or Milton.

Multiculturalism is married to the concept of globalism. Multiculturalism says that society should be tolerant of all cultures and that one's beliefs are no better or worse than others' opinions.

Multiculturalism expects a country to provide for an economic exchange with no assumed national mission and no particular people for whom the state exists. Multiculturalism says that this space belongs to everyone and, therefore, to no one in particular. In this hedonistic "Me generation," patriotism flies out the window.

Multiculturalists believe in cultural Marxism, which considers that all beliefs, customs, and ethics relate to the individual within that person's social context. In other words, "right" and "wrong" are culture-specific; there are no absolutes. What is considered moral in one society may be immoral in another. Since no universal standard of morality exists, no one can judge another person's beliefs. Once the community considered it healthy to have two genders, now if you believe this, you are vilified for being transphobic, which is a range of negative attitudes, feelings, or actions toward transgender people. Cultural Marxists have brought us closer to what George Orwell warned us where an omnipresent Party controls a totalitarian society whose three simple slogans are "War is Peace, Freedom is Slavery and Ignorance is Strength." Society forced Oceania to accept that two plus two may equal five if the Party deemed it so.

Multiculturalists believe that fake news is truth, submission is freedom, and diversity is strength. Some feminist movements even teach that boys can have periods so as not to distress transgender students. If you disagree, you are a despicable person who the mob will try to censor, get you fired from your job, humiliate you, shun you, and cancel you out for not subscribing to their dictates. Victims of this "cancel culture" can be statues of historical figures or even exhibits, as when the United Kingdom's Natural History Museum canceled its Darwin exhibits for being too "offensive." Any deviation from the orthodoxy is impermissible.

Multiculturalists care more about the equality of outcome where everyone should end up in the same place and less about opportunity and fairness. If there is inequality, it is the system's fault. Something unjust has happened, the regime has oppressed someone, so the system should protect and uplift disadvantaged groups and discriminate against advantaged groups.

Equality of outcome is rooted in Marxist ideology and the Communist Manifesto, where Karl Marx saw history as a struggle between oppressors and the oppressed. Multiculturalists believe that Marx failed because of his emphasis on economics, so they have taken Marxism from pure economics and married it to culture. Inequality exists because powerful social groups have oppressed weaker groups, so the system should correct this imbalance. If the law protects the privileged group, people should break the law.

A Dresden conference would typically attract hundreds of participants if it were not for a single person posting a tweet blaming bigotry organizers. There was not enough representation of minority groups and too many white male speakers. It did not matter that no discrimination occurred, and people of different genders and ethnicities had spoken in the past. It made no difference that the organizers received only one submission from a female out of hundreds. It did not matter that PHP is a language taught when there were few female programmers. What mattered was the accusation, which was sufficient to cause most speakers to withdraw from the conference. Subsequently, organizers canceled the event. When diversity and inclusion become more critical than substantive content, a meaningful exchange of ideas is doomed.

The term "racism" comes loaded with negative connotations because it suggests something evil, wrong, or immoral about a perceived favored group, such as white males of European heritage, standing up for their beliefs. Multiculturalists use the term to encourage one group to subordinate their interests to other groups under the threat of being accused of a "hate crime." Multiculturalism demands social justice and advocates safe spaces where people can go to evade criticism or unpleasant ideas. Multiculturalists discourage using certain "trigger words," sometimes called "negative feeling words," that might offend or make someone or a group feel uncomfortable. Even the songs 'Jingle Bells' and of course 'Baa Baa Black Sheep' are verboten. Quaker Foods has discontinued the Aunt Jemima brand and renamed it Pearl Milling Company, much to the dismay of the original Aunt Jemima family members. The measure in which society overcomes and corrects traditional social impediments is the new liberalism in a globalized society. Multiculturalists support equality laws to achieve social justice.

Buzzfeed, a leading digital media company, valued at $1.5 billion, published an article blaming white people for ruining America. The Root, an online media company owned by Univision with about 8 million visitors a month, has published articles accusing white privilege of many sins. In other words, multiculturalists believe that racism against white people can solve the problem of racism. Because multiculturalists assert that white people have historically dominated other groups, the system must suppress white people to equalize society.

There is no wisdom in people who fail to protect their culture, customs, and way of life. Why is there no wisdom? Because in secular societies, there is no God. Multiculturalists believe that people are born good, and therefore, God need not play a role. If people are not going to be accountable to God, they will put their faith in a central authority. It is not the government that has made people good in America; Biblical teachings have made good people. The secular world has brilliance and knowledge, but there is no wisdom because spiritual strength is necessary to have moral strength. Democratic and cultural values are not enough to save people from forces bent on destroying them. In a secular society, everything has to be watered down because of offenses, including the truth. Pope John Paul II called Europe, where secularism reigns supreme, the culture of death.

MULTIETHNIC

The 28-member European Union has come a long way since six European countries founded the European Economic Community in 1958. The founders aimed to avoid another devastating war in Europe by making its members economically interdependent. But what began as an economic union has turned globalist. Globalists have deceived Europeans into thinking that they have a voice in EU policies, but this is not the case.

The European Commission drafts legislation, and the European Parliament and the Council of Ministers make it legal. The EU court in Luxembourg interprets EU law and settles legal disputes. The EU can demand payment from the countries that do not comply with the court's rulings, but it has no real power because it cannot draft laws. The real power resides with the European Commission's unelected officials; who EU citizens cannot remove.

Multiculturalism has convinced educators to downplay history courses. America has been multiethnic but not multi-cultural. A multiethnic society accepts people from all cultures but expects them to integrate into the host country and live and adhere to its general beliefs and customs. Globalist ideas have transformed the Western world from being multiethnic to multi-cultural. Like Constantinople and Lebanon in earlier times, it is at risk of ethnocide by losing its cultural and ethnic identity. Multiculturalists support free speech, but the opinions of intolerant people and persons who speak out against the official narrative should not be allowed. When revolutionaries run out of monuments, they will burn churches. On July 4, 2020, there was a flag burning ceremony at the Gettysburg cemetery.

The opinion editor of the *New York Times* resigned after he apologized for publishing Arkansas senator Tom Cotton's call for deploying the military to quell riots in US cities during the unrest from the killing of George Floyd in 2020. Stan Wischnowski, the top editor of the *Philadelphia Inquirer*, resigned because he questioned the consequences of riots damaging the city's historic center. To avoid conflict, the Minneapolis City Council abolished the city's police department. New York City mayor Bill de Blasio announced he favors shifting funds from the police department to youth programs and social services. Hundreds of far-left protesters entered Seattle City Hall. They seized a six-block area in the Capitol Hill section of downtown, including an abandoned police precinct as Seattle leaders surrendered parts of the city to Antifa. Authorities' tepid response shows a lack of resolve to be the protectors of liberty.

ETHNOCIDE

Ethnocide is the deliberate and systematic destruction of national, ethnic, racial, or religious groups, such as white males. Ethnocide is the reason for the removal from the public view of historical statues. Cultural symbols that symbolize an ethnic culture, which some people construe as prejudice and racists, should be banned to neutralize the environment. Because the white race has dominated others, symbols of the white race are considered evil. The United Nations does not use the word "ethnocide" but uses the term "cultural genocide."

The multi-cultural model departs from the country's traditional view as a nation-state whereby the state or government exists to serve its nation or people. The Polish, Hungarians, the Czech Republic, and the Japanese understand that civilization is a pact between the dead, the living, and the unborn. However, lawmakers of most Western European countries have transformed themselves from a nation-state to a multi-cultural model favoring no particular people.

CHAPTER 3

WAR AGAINST FREEDOM

*T*he Cato Institute found that most Americans are afraid to reveal their core beliefs while censoring themselves from expressing political views, in some cases out of fear of losing their jobs or missing career opportunities, especially among conservatives. Even centrist liberals believe they must restrict themselves while only staunch liberals feel safe to voice their opinions. Even being a member of the far-right or far-left does not guarantee safety because purists will turn on anyone who is not radical enough.

WOKE MOVEMENT and CANCEL CULTURE

"Woke" means being aware and taking a stand against social injustice. Major corporations are now selling wokeness instead of their products. Pantene used to run commercials about shampoo; now, they show lesbian parents helping a biological boy become a girl. Dove celebrates women's different body types, and Vaseline portrays itself as fighting for equity in skincare. Oreo cookies have come out in support of the gay agenda, and Burger King takes a stance against bovine flatulence from cows as endangering the environment. Disney offers a diversity and inclusion program with affinity groups for minorities, but white employees are castigated for their whiteness. Penn State has moved towards wokemania by replacing the terms 'freshman' and 'senior' for not being gender inclusive. Companies now train employees in what it calls inclusion and diversity.

Freedom of conscience is the most important freedom we have, and a free and unbiased news media is essential to our liberty. But the social media giants are censoring more than ever because they have declared war on anything that is not politically correct, opinions that do not fit their world view. This sterilizing of the news has led to alternative news sources such as BitChute, Gab, Clouthub, Rokfin, Odysee, Lbry, Vimeo, MeWe, Parler, Rumble, and Frank. Frank is a social media platform providing a place for free speech as laid out in the U.S. Constitution. Mike Lindell says that the platform is like a combination of YouTube and Twitter. You don't get to use the four swear words—the C-word, the N-word, the F-word, or God's name in vain.

It will be difficult for these alternative news sources to compete with the tech giants' market power. YouTube estimates that 400 hours of video are uploaded every minute—making it mandatory to use algorithms and human moderation to scrutinize video content. YouTube demonetizes or delists videos regardless of the number of views. RT's English YouTube channel was issued a strike by the service over alleged Covid-19 disinformation. Some videos on RT's main English-language channel were made inaccessible for viewers for what YouTube said were violations of its policies on "medical misinformation" and "spam, deceptive practices, and scams." When YouTube gives a strike, it rarely explains the reason.

If YouTube gives you three strikes, it will ban you from the platform. YouTube gives strikes for copyright violations and for violating their community guidelines. If you get a copyright strike, it means that a copyright owner submitted a complete and valid legal takedown request for using their copyright-protected content. If you get a community guideline strike, it means your content violates YouTube's Community Guidelines. Only YouTube determines what those guidelines are. If you receive three strikes in the same 90-day period, YouTube will permanently remove your channel from the platform. Each strike will not expire until 90 days from the time it was issued.

The Texas Senate recently passed a bill that forbids social media companies that have at least 100 million users per month from blocking, banning, demonetizing, or discriminating against any of their users because of their political views. Other states are following the example.

Chad Robichaux is the founder of the Mighty Oaks Foundation, an organization that helps veterans overcome wartime trauma. When he tried to upload an ad for his organization, YouTube informed him that the keyword "Christian" was no longer acceptable; when he ran the same ad using the word "Muslim," YouTube accepted the video. When Suzanne Moore stated in an article, she wrote for *The Guardian* that "*Sex is not a feeling. Female is a biological classification that applies to all living species,*" the woke movement publically denounced this opinion, which led to the end of her 25-year tenure at the newspaper. Steve Thompson, a sports commentator, was suspended for using the term "handbag" on the air. The definition of a handbag is "an incident in which people, especially sportsmen, fight or threaten to fight but without real intent to inflict harm." Authorities forced a Swedish police reality show to delete a scene of children crying during a suspect's arrest.

Wokeness has descended upon the world like a blanket. At first, we could dismiss 'cancel culture' as a bad joke, but no one is laughing now. It is ironic that the Woke Movement began in the citadels of free thought and expression, college campuses. Today, many college students consider it their solemn duty to silence individuals who do not share their world views. Students have hurled rocks and torched buildings at the University of California as a protest against some conservative speakers. Kiersten Hening, a former

Virginia Tech college soccer star, was bullied, benched, and then forced off the team by her coach for her refusal to take the knee in supporting Black Lives Matter at intercollegiate events. Although she supports the general movement, she disagrees with the BLM organization, particularly its stance on defunding the police. She is suing her former coach for redresses. Greg Clarke, a chairman of the English Football Association, was forced to resign after misusing the word "color" when he talked about racism. He discussed how female and male football players are treated and stated that "colored" football players have to deal with more abuse. A colleague heard this and called him out on his use of the word.

As the Woke beast runs rampant across our culture, as a cultural civil war rages, purists consider your silence as an act of violence because not supporting some woke objective can be offensive. Some classics are now in danger, such as *Gone With the Wind, Song of the South, Path to 9/11, The Simpsons,* and *The Dukes of Hazard.* Because Harry Potter creator J.K. Rowling refuses to agree that a man can become a woman just by saying so, HBO Max has threatened to blacklist her Harry Potter franchise from its streaming service. In an action of modern-day book-burning, Target took the books *The End of Gender: Debunking the Myths about Sex and Identity in our Society* and *Irreversible Damage: The Transgender Craze Seducing Our Daughters* off its bookshelf because of one complaint. You can find a list of books that authorities have banned on the internet.

The Woke beast will always have to be fed by the changing landscape of political correctness. In the Supreme Court confirmation hearings, Amy Barrett mentioned the term "sexual preference." In response, Senator Mazie Hirono excoriated her for that term, claiming it was "offensive" to the LGBTQ community. That morning, "sexual preference" was an acceptable phrase. By lunchtime, the woke community deemed it "homophobic," and by sundown, it was so verboten that Merriam-Webster changed the definition to describe it as "offensive." In this Orwellian world, what you think about race, religion, disability, sexual orientation, transgender identity, and women can be criminalized under hate crime legislation. By introducing so-called "protected characteristics," the Scottish government plans to allow their courts to punish alleged "hate crimes" much more severely than other offenses by removing the burden of proof on the state when prosecuting an alleged hate crime. Instead, the "victims" opinion will be enough to convict someone of a "hate crime."

The documentary *The Social Dilemma* exposes the threat of technology where Silicon Valley insiders explain the danger that social media has over our lives. Many users are incapable of reading a book or distinguishing between fake news and real news. Directed by Jeff Orlowski, the video features interviews with former executives who created the technologies and business models in the early 2000s and believe that social media dehumanizes their customers, disrupts the social fabric, and destroys democracy. Orlowski argues that technology gives rise to severe social and political consequences because it is addictive, manipulative, and omnipresent. Social media has replaced actual human contact with abstract virtual connections that encourage selfishness, narcissism, and anti-social behavior, leading to increased depression, self-harm, and even suicide. Most of these executives disallow their children to participate in social media.

Negotiating life in this modern Woke culture can be tricky. When a teacher and mother of two children criticized LGBTQ teaching on Facebook, her employer fired her. Watch what you say, or the Woke police will pounce on you, and you will have no defense. When the owner of Palmetto Cheese, Brian Henry, criticized Black Lives Matter on Facebook, Costco eliminated the cheese in 120 stores. When Quinn Simmons, a world cycling champion, wrote a black hand emoji supporting President Trump on Twitter, the team leader benched him stating, *"While we support the right to free speech, we will hold people accountable for their words and actions."*

The British Labour leader Sir Keir Starmer prostrated himself before the gods of Woke to purge his soul of racism by taking an unconscious bias training course, complete with a certificate as proof of a passing grade. Twitter suspended Pennsylvania's State Senator Doug Mastriano's account for defending President Trump. Negotiating life in modern Woke culture requires real skill. Christians are fair game in this world of "all beliefs have equal value," even if it's a firmly held view borne of a deeply ingrained belief in the teachings of the Bible.

The banishment of Alex Jones from platforms was a turning point because when there was no conservative backlash, the left knew it was safe to discriminate against other right-wing commentators. Since then, Google has sanitized searches, and YouTube, Facebook, Instagram, and Twitter have de-platformed and demonetized right-wing programs. Even history teachers are suspended from YouTube for hate speech because they published Nazi Germany resources. Once we had a free market of competing and opposing ideas, we now have news and views dominated by the intellectual property complex. When an Oxford professor referred to a Danish study on Facebook that negated the effectiveness of face masks, fact-checkers flagged his post as false information. All of this censorship is taking a toll on people who do the censoring. A judge in California ruled that Facebook must pay 52 million dollars to moderators who developed post-traumatic stress disorder (PTSD).

Angela Davis is a left-wing activist who has been deeply involved in Communist politics, feminism movements, and other radical causes. Although Butler University scheduled her to be the lead speaker at a Joint Struggle and Collective Liberation event, the university canceled her appearance because she supported Palestinians. When Georgia passed a bill requiring voters to provide photo identification when they vote, Major League Baseball announced moving the All-Star Game from Atlanta to Denver, Colorado. United Airlines has abandoned merit-based hiring practices to appeal to the Woke Movement by notifying that fifty percent of pilot trainees will be women and minorities and Coca Cola admonishes their white employees to be less white. The US government has threatened to boycott the 2022 Beijing Olympics over China's Uighur Muslims treatment. The Cancel culture has convinced the Cleveland Indians baseball team to change its name after 100 years and convinced the actor Will Smith to relocate the filming of 'Emancipation' out of Georgia, citing the voting law as the reason.

In George Orwell's book *1984*, Winston Smith worked at the records department at the Ministry of Truth, where his job was to rewrite history according to big brother and party.

"And if all others accepted the lie which the Party imposed – if all records told the same tale—then the lie passed into history and became truth."

Winston believed that if the Ministry of Truth can alter a person's perception of the truth, then even a lie becomes the truth. Orwellian indoctrination can start as early as kindergarten with Critical Race Theory (CRT) indoctrinating youngsters with social justice teachings. CRT purports that society is inherently racist to further white people's interests. CRT teaches white children to dislike their roots, teaches black children that they are victims, and both are encouraged to be activists to right societies wrongs. With CRT either you are an exploiter (white) or a victim (black). CRT teaches children what to think rather than how to think. It was never about Confederate monuments; protesters have smashed statues of America's founding fathers and Christian icons. Even the nuclear family has come under attack as being rooted in Caucasian Judeo-Christian heritage. CRT is an attack on the core tenets of the Western value system; it turns the bedrock of traditional American ideals upside down.

Following is a quote from a letter written by a parent to other parents at Manhattan's Brearley private school.

> *"I object that the school is now fostering an environment where our daughters and teachers are afraid to speak their minds in class for fear of* "consequences." *I object that Brearley is trying to usurp the role of parents in teaching morality."*

Prager University filed a lawsuit to prevent YouTube from censoring its videos and discriminating against free speech, citing more than 80 videos that have been restricted or demonetized. For example, Google banned a video on "Thou Shall Not Kill" as being unsuited for young audiences, and YouTube has used "ideological discrimination" against some Prager U videos. Google, YouTube, and Facebook's policies have harmed the alternative news media and commentators such as Sarah Westall by censoring, demonetizing (taking advertising money away), delisting, deleting their programs for objectionable content, de-platformed (the canceling or disinviting someone), and shadow-banned others (secretly blocking content). When a YouTuber made a video to raise money to help victims of a tragedy, YouTube demonetized his channel because its policy is not to run ads about tragedies. When Nasim Aghdam had her YouTube channel NasimeSabz.com demonetized and censored, she drove to a YouTube headquarters and shot three people before killing herself. Is anyone safe in this era of wrongthink? Wrongthink is intolerant to dissent and leads to revisionist history.

The most dangerous censorship comes from the government, which collaborates with the media giants to rid their platforms of information contrary to the official narrative. Congress has summoned CEOs and told them they must toe the line or else. For example, opinions that the Twin Towers attack on 9-11 was an inside job is verboten. CEO Mark Zuckerberg had endorsed government censorship when he stated: "... *the question of what speech should be acceptable and what is harmful needs to be defined by regulation, by thoughtful governments.*" So the guardians of free speech have become the enemies of free speech, and the system has criminalized truth-seeking journalism. Facebook has altered its algorithms to align itself with government-funded think tanks to suppress opinions contrary to the official narrative. Twitter has banned some conservatives and anti-war activists and has partnered with the Orwellian *NewsGuard* "news rating" app, whose sole purpose is to drive viewers away from anti-establishment content.

Congress and the social media giants, such as Facebook and Twitter, have waged war against free speech under the guise of fighting fake news and supporting social justice. Only in this Orwellian World can YouTube award CEO Susan Wojcicki with the Freedom of Expression Award. In her acceptance speech, she speaks about how she is responsible for censoring its users by removing nine million videos over three months.

Whether we consider social media giants as platforms or publishers is the issue because the laws are very different. When the government regards social media as a platform, the companies are not responsible for content because they can hide behind Section 230 of the Communications Decency Act's legal protections. They cannot be sued, for example, if any defamatory content appears on their website. As platforms, they still have a responsibility for the content that violates federal criminal laws, but they can't be held responsible for misinformation or anyone espousing conspiracy theories, etc. But, the law removes these legal protections once they are considered publishers and not platforms. By controlling content, they act as publishers, but we grant them the freedom of platforms because Congress has not declared them publishers. Like the *New York Times*, a newspaper is considered a publisher and is therefore held liable for all content. Companies like Verizon and AT&T are platforms, they are not held responsible for what people say.

When Mark Zuckerberg claims that Facebook is both a publisher and a platform, he has the best of both worlds. Because Facebook has a notable bias towards liberal ideas and policies, it can discriminate against anyone who does not support left-leaning opinions. In this regard, it is acting as a publisher, like the *New York Times*. But because Congress allows it to operate as if it were a platform, Facebook is not held responsible for discriminating against ideas contrary to its belief system—it has the freedom to censor anyone it wishes. It controls the narrative. Although Congress passed Section 230 to promote a free and open internet, Facebook, Twitter, and Google now use it to advocate for an open internet while at the same time justifying censorship. As publishers, they could not discriminate, but as platforms, they have unfettered freedom.

In a perfect world, Congress would have prevented the concentration of power by applying US antitrust law to social media's anticompetitive behavior. If the Justice Department had used the "concentration of power," the government would have prevented Google from buying YouTube and DoubleClick, Facebook Instagram, and Microsoft LinkedIn. But the plan is to give these tech giants unfettered global power in cyberspace so that governments can partner with them to control the narrative. According to the Pew Research Center, more than two-thirds of people receive their news from social media. A left-leaning organization, The Southern Law Center, is assisting YouTube in policing content. Censorship is a big issue when 90% of what we watch, listen to, and read is owned by only six companies, News Corp, Disney, Viacom, Time Warner, CBS, and Comcast; in 1993, it was fifty companies.

Twitter systematically purges offensive terms in the name of political correctness. The term "man hours" has been replaced with "person hours" and "grandfathered" with "legacy status." Twitter has replaced the words "master" and "slave" with the terms "leader" and "follower." SEAL's now use words such as "warriors" and "citizens" rather than "brothers" or "men." The Associated Press capitalizes "Black" but does not capitalize "white." Facebook and Google have partnered with Politifact and Snopes to mark what they consider false information. Facebook claims that they will de-emphasize anyone without meaningful interactions, and only it can determine what is "a meaningful interaction." Publishers like BuzzFeed, who publish social and lifestyle content, qualify for preferential treatment over news publishers, and YouTube uses a spell check for hate speech. Opinions contrary to the established narrative are discouraged and labeled fake news. In Germany, Facebook, Twitter, and other social media companies face up to 50 million euros ($57 million) for failing to remove hate speech within 24 hours. Social networks have to publish reports every six months detailing how many complaints they received and how they dealt with them, and the European Council requires web companies to block hate speech videos.

MASS SURVEILLANCE

Microsoft agreed to divulge their customer's records beyond what the law required beginning in 2007. Next came Yahoo in 2008, Google, Facebook in 2009, YouTube in 2010, Skype in 2011, and Apple in 2012. This process is called "Upstream Collection" or "Upstream Agreement" from these companies to the National Security Agency (NSA). The Tech titans employ surveillance-based models that threaten human rights and erode privacy without fear of prosecution because of the Protect America Act of 2008, which protects media companies from prosecution by customers who might sue them for exposing personal information.

Smith versus Maryland is a court case in the 1970s where a man was making harassing phone calls to a woman. She was able to get his license plate number and went to the police. The police went to the phone company and said: "*In this case, we do not have a warrant, but we do have this guy's license plate number, will you give us his telephone records anyway?*" The phone company agreed. The Supreme Court ruled that this person did not have a right to privacy because the authorities did not listen to his telephone conversations-it only revealed who he called and when. Lawyers call this the Third-Party Doctrine; it opened the door for the government to have surveillance on everyone, everywhere, and forever. If the government can collect one person's phone calls without a warrant, it can receive everyone's phone calls, emails, social media posts, etc., without authorization.

CRIMINALIZING FREE SPEECH

European Governments have criminalized free speech and have imprisoned people for violating laws that forbid the voicing of some opinions. A judge in Austria sentenced Dr. Georg Zakrajsek to five months in prison for claiming that Islam has declared war on the Western world. Nigel Pelham of Sussex, England, was sentenced to 20 months in jail for posting his opinions about Islam on Facebook. France sentenced a man to two years in prison for making a blog post aimed against Islamization. Michael Hess of Sweden had to pay a 32,000 Kroner fine for "hate speech" after writing about rape statistics. England has jailed a former soldier for a speech where he incited people to free England from Jewish control. *"This is England, and this is our land... We want our country back, and we are going to take it back."* German police have raided people's homes over social media posts that allegedly contained offensive content. Scotland seeks to eradicate the distinction between citizens' private lives and public life by making it a crime to use any form of hate speech in one's private home.

Canada's hate speech laws cover public communications that promote hatred by gender identity or gender expression. Turkey's parliament has ratified a bill compelling major social media companies to delete content deemed offensive. According to Mark Zuckerberg, Facebook censors almost 90 percent of "hate speech" before it is allowed to circulate. There is no universal agreement on what constitutes hate speech; the ruling authority decides in each case. Chapter 15, Section 8 of Sweden's criminal code prohibits the expression of "disrespect" towards favored minority groups with a penalty of up to four years' imprisonment. The law requires no evidence of incitement to violence and lacks any objective standard for identifying "disrespect." A Swedish appeals court overturned the conviction of Pastor Ake Green, the first clergyman convicted under the law, citing free speech protections. The original court sentenced Pastor Green to one month in jail for a sermon that he preached to his congregation on Biblical texts addressing homosexuality. Let this sink in; authorities imprison a pastor for referring to the Bible!

CULTURAL RELATIVISM

Freedom of expression flies out the window when people can't speak their minds. The United Nations General Assembly proclaimed the Universal Declaration on Human Rights in 1948, and the UN adopted the International Covenant on Civil and Political Rights in 1966. Both declarations guaranteed the right to freedom of expression.

"Everyone shall have the right to hold opinions without interference, and everyone

shall have the right to freedom of expression."

"Everyone has the right to freedom of opinion and expression; this right includes freedom to hold opinions without interference and to seek, receive and impart information through any media and regardless of frontiers."

Despite laws that protect free speech, countries have declared war on free speech when opinions are contrary to cultural relativism. Cultural relativists believe that all cultures have value, even those with conflicting moral beliefs. A diversity of cultures requires no agreement on what is considered right and wrong or good and evil. Scottish authorities have disciplined police officers for engaging in private conversations on WhatsApp deemed racist, sexist, anti-Semitic, homophobic, and mocking of the disabled, completing a house of taboo subjects. Officers argued that they have a right to privacy under Article 8 of the European Convention of Human Rights and common law. But the court ruled that "the onus on those officers to uphold the force's rules and protect the public overrode their right of privacy." Do we, as private citizens, have a right to freedom of thought and speech, even in private conversations? The officers' discussions took place on a private encrypted WhatsApp group.

Even casual comments can lead to unpredictable results. When the president of Princeton University, Christopher Eisgruber, wrote a letter decrying the university's racism, the Department of Education launched an investigation of the university. If found guilty, the university could lose millions of dollars in aid from the federal government. The Department issued a formal request looking for racist practices in violation of the Civil Rights Act of 1964. The act states that no person *"on the ground of race, color, or national origin, be excluded from participation in, be denied the benefits of, or be subjected to discrimination under any program or activity receiving financial assistance."* The incident that led to the investigation was when Eisgruber revealed his concern for anti-black racism in America and its direct effect on the university. *"Racism and the damage it does to people of color persist at Princeton and racist assumptions are imbedded in the structures of the university itself."* So his admitted racism at Princeton is what led to the investigation. The Education Department's letter to the university, *"Based on admitted racism, the US Department of Education is concerned Princeton's nondiscrimination and equal opportunity assurances in its Program Participation Agreements from at least 2013 to the present may have been false."* in another case, Arizona State University offered Sonya Duhe a dean position. But when she posted a tweet saying she was praying for the family of George Floyd and the "good police officers that keep us safe," the university canceled its offer stating that she was fomenting "microaggressions."

Globalism in Western Europe has led to a loss of national purpose and identity; Europeans are beginning to mourn their loss of independence because Europe is on its cultural deathbed. Canada's multi-cultural policies are pushing it down the same path. The Canadian legislature changed the country's 1908 national anthem by replacing the words *"in all thy sons command"* with *"in all of us command"* to make the song more gender-neutral—the offending terms referenced men killed in World War I. Europe and Canada are moving away from nationalism toward globalism.

Globalists believe that only a central authority can solve humanity's problems. Instead of being a citizen of a country, we should become citizens of the world. Under globalism, there is the erasure of culture, ethnicity, and European heritage. A global citizen typically favors population reduction, income equality, open borders, centralized education, gun control, and vaccines. Globalists utilize the divide and conquer strategy; they instigate anarchy wherever they can, undermine the free market system wherever possible, and stoke fears of looming disasters, such as foreign enemies, global warming, and pandemics.

WAR AGAINST CRITICAL THINKING

Public education is going through the throes of revisionist history favoring more civics, sociology, and feel-good courses. The teaching of America being founded by white Christian men and emphasizing slavery as the central issue of the War of Succession paints a picture of white supremacy over blacks. Therefore, some school systems abolish this viewpoint from their textbooks, especially those who have agreed to Common Core. Common Core is a set of learning standards that have influenced a whole generation to value fairness over opportunity and rote memory over cognitive thinking.

The US Department of Education put out a memo in July of 2009 which stated,

> *"President Barack Obama and US Secretary of Education Arne Duncan today announced that states leading the way on school reform will be eligible to compete for $4.35 billion in Race to the Top competitive grants to support education reform and innovation in classrooms."*

Once a state accepts the money, they have to abide by the Common Core standards. An early backing of the Common Core proposal came from the Bill and Melinda Gates Foundation. The foundation spread money across the political spectrum, including the teacher's unions, the American Federation of Teachers and the National Education Association, and business organizations such as the US Chamber of Commerce. Money flows to groups who promote standards that support cultural relativism. To control the global media narrative, since 2000, the foundation has donated more than $45 billion to "charitable causes."

Bill Gates and others like him are technocrats; they may be interested in education, but they are more interested in power and control. They see technology as a way to influence people's opinions about fairness, the environment, and population control—they want to shape the world through their beliefs and to replace cognitive thinking with sociology and ideology under the guise of "social justice." When the Gates Foundation hired lobbyists, they influenced Congress to overreach into the area of public education. We now have a system that demands uniformity—schools teach children to fear decent from the mainstream narrative and be intolerant of opposing viewpoints.

Government mandating schools to teach gender identity issues and homosexual marriage would have been inconceivable years ago. Now, not only is it accepted, but authorities consider students regressive if they disagree with this liberal teaching. The Every Student Succeeds Act weaves alternative lifestyle education into every subject; even math uses story problems dealing with the topic! The National Sexuality Education Standards web page states, *"The National Sexuality Education Standards is to provide clear, consistent and straightforward guidance on the essential minimum, core content for sexuality education that is age-appropriate for public school students in grades K-12."* The government activated these standards along with the Common Core curriculum in public schools.

Rachel Carson Middle School in Herndon, Virginia, is full of winners. The school won a governor's award for teaching excellence from 2007 to 2011, and the national forum for middle-school improvement cited Rachel Carson as a school to watch. However, the federal government considers the school a failure because it does not fit its success definition to improve test scores of different groups. Carson has high average scores but fails because it has achievement gaps when it breaks out test results by categorizing race, gender, and income.

WAR AGAINST PRIVATE COLLEGES

Corinthian College was a college with more than 100 campuses. Private colleges, like Corinthian, specialize in training students for blue-collar jobs, jobs such as driving big commercial trucks, nursing, cloud computing, web development, database programming, software development, and network security by offering degrees in healthcare, business, criminal justice, transportation, construction trades, and information technology. Corinthian was a for-profit college and one of the largest for-profit post-secondary education companies in North America. Because the college failed to meet government mandates promptly, the Department of Education put it out of business. The federal government restricted its access to federal funding because of its inadequate marketing, excessive dropouts and student loan default rates, and unfulfilled promises. Because 80% of Corinthians' revenue came from federal funding, $1.4 billion in federal financial aid each year, the lack of funding was a death blow. Consumer Financial Protection Bureau (CFPB) wiped out company shareholders and creditors by accusing the college of predatory lending. It claimed that Corinthian used aggressive collection efforts by suspending students who failed to meet their loan obligations and paying staff bonuses for collecting past-due payments, and a shortage of graduates finding full-time employment in their chosen field.

Another casualty is the ITT Technical Institute; the institute operated a profit college with 130 campuses in 38 states and was operational for 50 consecutive years. On September 26, 2016, ITT abruptly shut down, leaving 35,000 students without a degree and 8,000 employees without a job. The closure is the same as with Corinthian College; the Department of Education claimed that ITT was charging tens of thousands of dollars in tuition but failing to provide valuable education.

A third casualty occurred in June of 2016 when the Department of Education (DOE) forced the Accrediting Council for Independent Colleges and Schools (ACICS) to close by suspending its accreditation. ACICS was the most comprehensive accrediting agency of for-profit colleges and universities with 245 colleges and 800,000 students. The department accused ACICS of not spending taxpayer dollars effectively and is now judging all colleges and universities on graduation and retention rates, graduates' ability to pay back their student loans, the school's accessibility to low-income students, and their ability to hold down costs.

The Tenth Amendment of the US Constitution reads, *"The powers not delegated to the United States by the Constitution, nor prohibited by it to the States, are reserved to the States respectively, or to the people."* Therefore, the Tenth Amendment leaves the power to create schools and a system for education in the hands of individual states, not the federal government. But the federal government has ignored this fact and has waged war against the freedom to choose.

ANTI-ZIONISM vs. ANTI-SEMITISM

Authorities use anti-Zionism and anti-Semitism laws to suppress the freedom of thought and speech. Zionism is an ideology and a political movement to establish the Jewish nation in Palestine. Zionists seek a Biblical homeland because they believe that Jews deserve their ancestral land as promised in the Old Testament. Zionism makes any hostility against the politics of modern day Israel anti-Semitic.

America has laws against anti-Semitism, laws against hatred of the Jewish people, and is now criminalizing Zionism's criticism. Florida's governor signed a bill making it a crime to speak out against the Israeli government. Laws against anti-Semitism protect a group of people; laws against anti-Zionism defend the government of Israel. These laws equate criticism of Zionism with anti-Semitism and infringe on free speech by making opinions contrary to Zionism unlawful.

The Global Anti-Semitic Act of 2004 directs the Secretary of State to submit an annual report to Congress documenting anti-Semitic acts. Any assertion that Jews control the government, the media, international business, and the financial world is considered anti-Semitic. The law blurs the line between what is anti-Israel and anti-Semitic. If a person speaks out against Israel's policies toward the Palestinians, that person is considered an anti-Semite. Any criticism of the US government for being under the Jewish-Zionist community's influence, including AIPAC, is anti-Semitic. Any person who associates the Jewish community with the New World Order the State Department considers that person an anti-Semite. The law labels anyone who proclaims that Jewish leaders influenced Rome to crucify Christ an anti-Semite. Any person who claims that the Mossad, the National Intelligence Agency of Israel, was behind the 9/11 attack on the Twin Towers is an anti-Semite. Anti-Semitism is a hate crime in many countries, and the US State Department equates "strong, anti-Israel sentiment" and criticism of matters Jewish with "hate." Such directives open the door to persecuting people who criticize Israel's policies as domestic terrorists.

ANTI-DEFAMATION LEAGUE

The Anti-Defamation League, ADL, is a pro-Israel group that considers criticism of Israel to be anti-Semitic. ADL has developed an online hate index to recognize hate speech and targets it for censorship. The aim is to establish a worldwide pro-Israel network and is the first call for anti-Semitism. The online hate index identifies trends and patterns in hate speech across different months and gathers intelligence on activist groups to counter their efforts. *Fortune* magazine reported that Facebook, Google, and YouTube are complying with up to 95% of Israeli requests to delete content favorable to the Palestinians.

AIPAC AND FREE SPEECH

American Israeli Political Action Committee (AIPAC) was founded in 1963 and is the largest pro-Israel lobbying group in Washington. It pours tens of millions of dollars each year into the pockets of politicians expecting pro-Israel legislation. The government fired Stephen Rosen from AIPAC because he used his contacts to spy for the Israeli government. Rosen was so upset that he filed a lawsuit arguing that the government should not have fired him because Israeli spying was so common; the court dropped all charges against him. The Democratic Majority for Israel is another lobbying group that advocates pro-Israel policies.

Cynthia McKinney was the first African woman to represent Georgia in the House of Representatives. When she first arrived in Congress, AIPAC presented her with a pledge (a paragraph) stating her support. If Cynthia signed the pledge, AIPAC would give her financial and personnel support. Because Cynthia did not sign the pledge, AIPAC forced her out of Congress. In 1990, six-term Congressman Gus Savage gave an hour-long speech in Congress. He detailed how AIPAC subverts the democratic process on behalf of Israel. Congress forced him out by accusing him of being an anti-Semite. Representative James Traficant was critical of AIPAC when Congress expelled him. A federal judge sentenced him to eight years in prison and fined him $150,000 following his conviction on ten counts of bribery, racketeering, and tax evasion. Congress has equated speaking out against the policies of AIPAC equivalent to anti-Semitism and touching the third rail. The third rail is a topic that is so controversial that it would immediately damage one's political career.

BDS

Israel's military has controlled the West Bank since the 1967 War. However, most countries do not recognize the legality of Israel's claim and accept the territory as Palestinian. Boycott Divestment and Sanctions (BDS) was launched in 2005 by Palestinian organizations to stop Israel from building houses illegally in occupied territories. The BDS movement has three primary goals:

1. End the Israeli occupation of Palestinian land by dismantling the security wall through the West Bank.
2. Palestinians should have the legal rights of Jews.
3. Let Palestinian refugees return to their homes as stipulated by the 1948 United Nations Resolution 194.

The United Nations General Assembly and not the Security Council adopted the resolution, and, therefore, the declaration is not binding. The BDS movement encourages individuals and organizations to boycott companies that have business dealings with Israel.

Officials in 26 states have imposed restrictions on people who back BDS, and anti-BDS legislation has passed at least half of US state legislatures. In Florida, you are prevented from state contracts if you support BDS. You do not qualify for hurricane relief funding in Texas if you do not sign an anti-BDS pledge; a speech pathologist lost her job at a Texas school for not signing an anti-BDS pledge.

Andrew Cuomo, the Governor of New York, announced: *"If you boycott against Israel, New York will boycott you."* He then signed an executive order requesting a list of organizations who *"participate in boycott, divestment, or sanctions activity targeting Israel."* New Jersey, Illinois, and others have passed laws divesting their pension funds from companies backing BDS. The House Foreign Affairs Committee unanimously passed legislation named the "Israel Anti-Boycott Act," which prohibits companies from participating in boycotts that target US partners, such as Israel.

CHAPTER 4

PITCHFORKS

*W*hen a policeman killed George Floyd in June of 2020, people demanded a change in the status quo. They staged violent protests against racism, police brutality and railed against the injustice done against black people. The protests started peacefully, but eventually, other rioters came out to destroy property and harm people; these are the Jacobins. Kay Boulton, a white woman who moved to Minneapolis from Michigan to attend law school, was arrested and spent 16 hours in jail. She described herself as philosophically an anarchist but not a revolutionary. She is a typical Jacobin. The name comes from a radical political group during the French Revolution of 1789. The word "terrorist" comes from the reign of terror the Jacobins waged during the French Revolution. Some rioters are Jacobins, they react out of anger, and they wish to destroy the present system, but they do not have a plan to replace it with something better.

Marxists have a vision of replacing capitalism with communism, but this is all theory; they do not specify how a central authority would produce and distribute goods and services. Marxism is a social and political philosophy named after Karl Marx. In his book *Das Kapital*, Marx divided society into two main groups, the proletariat, and the bourgeoisie. The bourgeoisie owns the means of production, and the proletariat has nothing to sell but labor. As time goes on, the bourgeoisie will grow wealthier as the disparity in income increases. Eventually, the proletariat overthrows the bourgeoisie in a revolution and establishes a classless society called communism. In the early years of the Soviet Union, Lenin and Stalin designed a communist economic system where central planning replaced the price mechanism.

Whereas Marx saw society as a conflict between the bourgeoisie and the proletariat, the working class, and the capitalist class, the Frankfurt School replaced the communist movement. Because the early communists failed to get enough support from factory workers, they decided to expand their base by appealing to every oppressed person. The issue became the conflict between white people, primarily white heterosexual males, and everyone else. Not only is it a conflict aimed at white people, but it is against the history, institutions, and shared beliefs of Western civilization, thus the destruction of statues that represent a history of Western civilization. Cultural Marxism says that there is no "right" and "wrong," there are no absolutes, but everything is culture-specific, and that free speech should be reserved for the oppressed class, but not to the oppressor class. Thus we get attacks against free speech on university campuses because cultural Marxists believe they are taking the moral high ground. Destruction is a crucial element of the modern Marxist movement, money creation is always the answer to a decline in economic activity, and the only real power is political. Social Marxism says that in the pursuit of equality, the system has to treat groups unequally.

George Soros, Twitter CEO Jack Dorsey, and other people fund Black Lives Matter (BLM) and other Marxist groups. Dorsey has donated ten million dollars to the Kendi's Center for Antiracist Research. According to an interview that CNN did with BLM founder Patrisse Cullors on January 20, 2020, she is a communist and a trained organizer of Marxist ideology. Hawk Newsome, head of Black Lives Matter of Greater New York, told Fox News anchor Martha MacCallum he wants to burn down the system if the system does not satisfy black needs. Susan Rosenberg, a communist and a person who spent 16 years in prison for terrorist activities against the United States, serves on the board for Thousand Currents, responsible for the global fund-raising efforts of Black Lives Matter.

Protests may be peaceful until Antifa shows up. Antifa is short for anti-fascist; they are against fascism and wish to replace it with some vague communist notion. Under fascism, there is private property, the freedom to buy and sell, the profit motive, and free elections. But the system centralizes authority in the hands of a few wealthy persons. In most fascists societies, citizens believe that they live in a democracy; they are not aware that a nefarious group controls them.

The Sunrise Movement, funded by the Rockefeller Foundation, is active in schools encouraging students to join the war against fascism. It wants our energy system of fossil fuels replaced with wind and solar while building an army of young people to make climate change an urgent priority across America. Sunrise convinces students that support for programs, such as the Green New Deal, is about climate change. Still, in reality, it is about replacing democracy with communism. It is like a watermelon, green on the outside and red on the inside. Their website explains how communism will fix the problem of white supremacy and the uneven distribution of wealth. The US Department of Homeland Security is now providing $10 million in grants to organizations that combat white supremacy.

UNEVEN DISTRIBUTION OF WEALTH

The Gini Index is a statistical measure of income distribution developed by the Italian statistician Corrado Gini in 1912. The lower the index, the more equal a country's income distribution. According to the World Bank, the US score in 1979 was 34.6, and in 2016 it was 41.5. The poor can sometimes make more money by not working, and the system rewards the wealthy, but the middle class pays the piper. According to the Brookings Institute, 53 million people between the ages of 18 and 64, who represent 44 percent of the US workforce, fall in the category of "low wage." Their hourly pay averages $10.22, and the median annual earning is $18,000. The majority are adults in their prime working years, and the low pay is primary to supporting their families. The study found that these statistics hold up in the majority of regions across the United States. The average real wage has the same purchasing power as it did in 1980.

Low wages for the middle class benefit lenders because they force people to borrow and use their homes as ATMs. A sure way to go broke is to ask, "what's the monthly payment?" The Baby-Boom generation led the Millennials to live beyond their means by buying houses they can't afford and SUVs they don't need. Politicians convinced people that owning a home is the American dream, but what they meant is that debt can make you feel prosperous as an indentured servant. The artificially low-interest rates has led to a systemic breakdown. They have been a bonanza for wealthy investors but have robbed others of a decent return on their savings. Debt is the money of slaves.

While the circus continues, the bread is thinning out, except for the top 0.001%. The middle has fallen out of the middle class as it disappears into a black hole of debt. The Gallup poll asked people, what class they belonged to, lower class, middle class or upper class? In 2000, 31 percent of Americans answered the lower class; by 2016, 49 percent responded that they were in the lower class. According to Oren Case at the Manhatten Institute, the typical American man needs 53 weeks to pay for the basics of middle-class family life, while for a single female, it takes 66 weeks to make ends meet. According to the School Nutrition Association, there are 22 million children who depend on free or reduced-price school lunch as their daily nutrition, and the US Census Bureau has found that only persons with at least a bachelor's degree have progressed. Nearly half of Americans depend on the government to survive.

We have been robbed of our prosperity and freedom by endless wars, debt, taxes, corrupt politicians, and laws that inhibit our freedom of speech and right of assembly. When people realize that the same special interest groups control both political parties, their anger and frustration will demand change. The growing disparity of income between the haves and have nots has exposed corporate greed, and greed digs the deepest grave. We live in a political system ruled by the few. Warren Buffett, who is worth billions, has often said that we are in a class war, and his class is winning!

PITCHFORKS

Nick Hanauer was the first non-family investor in Amazon and sold another company to Microsoft for 6.4 billion dollars. He credits his success to a good intuition about the future. He asks, *"What do I see in the future? Pitchforks, as in angry mobs with pitchforks against the super-rich."* While the one percent prospers, the ninety-nine percent are falling behind. The problem is not that we have some inequality; a capitalistic society needs some inequality; the problem is that inequality is grossly uneven. At a meeting with Goldman Sachs bankers, Mike Bloomberg, who is worth sixty billion dollars, stated: *"People will turn to guillotines if we do not find jobs for the poor."*

Ray Dalio is the founder of Bridgewater Associates, the world's largest hedge fund. He believes that people with pitchforks will be coming after him and others like him because capitalism has worked for him, but not so much for others. He talks about how wages have been stagnant since the 1980s, while the top earners' wealth has increased. Dalio believes that the exclusion of youth from prosperity, anger against the growing disparity gap, an unjust system, a concern about the future, unemployment, and changing values will lead to riots and possible revolution. Although, you may not read the word "riot" because the Associated Press (AP) has issued a new set of

Orwellian guidelines that cautions against using the term to avoid stigmatizing groups protesting for racial justice.

CHAPTER 5

GHOULS OF DECEPTION

A false flag concocts a crisis, stirs a reaction, then proposes a solution that will convince people to agree to a policy that they would otherwise not support. Perpetrators of false flags are masters of deception. A false flag event will stir emotions, then followed by a news blitz. Shortly after, authorities will identify a scapegoat with little or no concrete facts to back up the accusation. The higher the shock value, the more spectacular the event, the more people killed, the more severe the unemployment and bankruptcies, the fewer people will question the authenticity of the occurrence.

The term comes from the old days of wooden ships when a ship would hang the flag of its enemy before attacking one of its own—then it would blame the enemy for the attack and thereby gain public support. One of the most ominous false flag events is one that never materialized. Operation Northwoods was a series of false-flag proposals that originated with the CIA in 1962 but were rejected by the Kennedy administration. The CIA proposed acts of terrorism in US cities blaming Cuba to instigate public support for a war against that nation. There need not be an actual incident to initiate a false flag. In 1964, two American ships claim they were attacked by the Vietnamese in the Gulf of Tonkin. Even though President Johnson knew the attacks were unfounded, he used it as a false flag to wage war against Viet Nam without Congressional approval. The National Security Agency in 2005 confirmed that the attack never took place.

False flag perpetrators influence public opinion by controlling the news. One sign that an incident is a false flag is an exaggerated coverage of the occurrence over an extended time by the news media. Sometimes an event occurs that is not a prearranged false flag, but authorities use the incident anyway. The assassination of Archduke Ferdinand in Sarajevo in 1914 could be a case in point. The killing may not have been pre-planned as an excuse to start a world war, but it was an excuse for the war. Dr. Mikovits, the author of the film *"Plandemic,"* believes that COVID-19 is nothing more than severe flu that has been used as a false flag incident to spread panic worldwide. The top official at Russia's state health watchdog believes that there is no point in suspending the economy to fight COVID-19 and bars, restaurants, and shops should remain open.

The Swedish King Gustav III was looking for a way to unite his country in the 1780s. He decided that a war with Russia would be just the thing. So he dressed some of his men in Russian military uniforms and attacked a Swedish military post along the Russian border. The ruse worked, and the people supported a war with Russia. In 1931, Japan was looking for an excuse to invade Manchuria, so Japan detonated TNT along a Japanese railway in the Manchurian city of Mukden. Blaming the Manchurians for the attack, people supported a war. When authorities exposed the deception, ministers forced Japan to withdraw from the League of Nations. Adolph Hitler burned down the Reichstag, the German parliament, in 1933 and blamed it on the communists.

The award-winning documentary *Loose Change 9/11: An American Coup* starts with the Reichstag event. The burning of the Reichstag (parliament) building in Berlin on the night of February 27, 1933, was an event contrived by the newly formed Nazi government to turn public opinion against its opponents. The following day the government passed the Reichstag Fire Decree, also called the Decree for the Protection of People and the Reich, blaming the communists for the fire. The Decree suspended most civil liberties and banned publications considered unfriendly to the Nazi cause. Hitler then took control of the German Parliament and pushed through the Enabling Acts, and began his invasion of neighboring countries, starting with Poland.

Israel's attack on the *USS Liberty* in 1967 was a false flag event that almost brought America into a war against Egypt. The term that describes these events is "casus belli," a Latin term defined as "an event or action that justifies or allegedly justifies a war or conflict." On June 8, 1967, during the Six-Day War, Israel attacked the unarmed and marked *USS Liberty Ship* with over 5,000 armor-piercing bullets, napalm, and five torpedoes (only one hit the ship). The *USS Liberty* was the most sophisticated intelligence-gathering ship in the US Navy. When the vessel tried to send out SOS signals for help, the messages were jammed—the attackers had to know the secret codes and radio frequency to jam the signals. Afterward, the Israeli jets came back to finish off the survivors. One radioman on the *USS Saratoga*, an aircraft carrier in the area, engaged in war games, picked up an SOS signal from the Liberty on an open circuit frequency. Upon contacting the authorities, the admiral sent jets to help the ship. But soon after, a higher power recalled the aircraft. The admiral ordered the second wave of planes, and again Robert MacNamara ordered a recall. When the admiral asked for a higher authority, President Lyndon Johnson got on the phone, stating that "*I will not embarrass an ally over a few dead sailors.*" Johnson allowed 16 hours before he gave the go-ahead to rescue the Liberty and provide aid to the wounded sailors.

TruNews has made a movie about the *USS Liberty* with the help of the survivors named *"Sacrificing Liberty."* Go to https://www.sacrificingliberty.com/ to purchase the video. The following is a quote from the back jacket of the four disk collection.

> "*The* USS Liberty *was deliberately sent into the kill zone. The casualties were staggering: 34 killed and 174 wounded. The cover-up began immediately and has continued since 1967. Until now! The aging survivors have finally told their true story.* Sacrificing Liberty *sets the record straight.*"

The Lavon affair was a failed Israeli Mossad covert operation, codenamed Operation Susannah, conducted in Egypt in 1954. As part of the false flag operation, many Egyptian Jews planted bombs inside American, Egyptian, and British libraries. It made it look like the Muslim Brotherhood planted the bombs. The purpose was to induce the British government to retain its occupying troops in Egypt's Suez Canal zone. If Americans believed that the Egyptians did it, they would turn against Egypt. The operation became known as the Lavon Affair after the Israeli defense minister Pinhas Lavon.

False flags manipulate citizens by placing fear in their hearts. Whether you accept the official story of 9-11 or believe it was a staged event, there is no dispute about what happened afterward. The occurrence led to the Patriot Act, which empowered the federal government while lessening personal liberties. By ushering in the war on terror, it enticed Americans to trade freedom for security.

STOVEPIPING AND GASLIGHTING

Stovepiping is similar to false flags. Whereas a false flag uses an incident to convince people to take action, stovepiping uses incorrect information to sway public opinion. For example, false information and media cooperation over two years led to the Russiagate panic. The Mueller investigation found no evidence that the Russians meddled in the 2016 presidential election, but the accusation impacted people's perception of events. All it took for the US to invade Iraq in 2003 was the false accusation that Iraq possessed weapons of mass destruction.

Gaslighting sows seeds of doubt in a person or a group, hoping to make them question their memory or cherished beliefs. The term "Gaslighting" comes from a 1938 play by Patrick Hamilton. Throughout the play, the abusive husband, Gregory, manipulates Paula to believe she has gone mad. He leads her to think she's stealing things without realizing it and hearing noises that are not there. Paula begins to question her sanity. Gaslighting hides truths from victims and allows perpetrators control. Social Media gaslights millennials by convincing them that living with their parent's house forever is fine. Generation Z is encouraged to lower their expectations and ditch their dreams of financial independence as the economy circles the drain.

CHAPTER 6

MERCHANTS OF DEATH

*I*t should be evident to anyone who is paying attention that the world is on the cusp of radical change. We are witnessing the beginning of a global banking dictatorship where a universal digital currency will supplant national currencies and mark the end of liberty. This transition will complete the demise of freedom except for a privileged few.

President Woodrow Wilson and Congress gave up control over the money supply when it transferred authority from the government to the world private banking cabal with the Federal Reserve Act of 1913. At about the same time, when Czar Nicholas Romanov refused to cooperate with the world bankers, the cabal engineered a revolution in 1917 to topple the monarchy, establish a new government and install a central bank under its control. Nicholas was not only a stumbling block to establishing a Russian central bank, but he was also aware of the banker's plot of world domination. The Bolsheviks did not only kill the Czar; they also killed all the members of the Russian Royal family, including women and children. In 1922, Lenin formed a dictatorship under communism and renamed the government the Union of Soviet Socialist Republics. Since 1972 Russia has been able to free itself from the banking cabal's grasp, gain its independence, and establish a Christian nation once again.

CURRENCIES

Commercial banks can multiply money, but only central banks can create money. Before the banking system can multiply money, someone has to make a deposit. But the Federal Reserve does not need a deposit; it can create money by merely pushing a few keys on its computer to credit a client's account by X amount. All currencies are debt instruments; they are floating abstractions that profit the world's bankers. At the top of a dollar bill is printed "Federal Reserve Note." A note is an IOU; it is an agreement to pay interest to the Federal Reserve. Dollars come into existence when the government sells bonds to the Federal Reserve. Therefore, we pay interest to the bankers. The Bureau of Engraving and Printing converts only a tiny fraction of this borrowed money into physical dollars.

A cartel of eight families owns the Federal Reserve and other central banks around the world. They are Goldman Sachs of New York, Rockefeller Brothers of New York, Rothschild Banks of London and Berlin, Lazard Brothers of Paris, Israel Moses Sieff Banks of Italy, Kuhn and Loeb and Company of Germany and New York, and the Warburg Bank of Hamburg and Amsterdam. The Federal Reserve is listed in the telephone book's white pages, while the US Treasury is listed in the yellow pages. Fed employees' email address ends in .org, not .gov.

Starting with Mayer Amschel Rothschild (1743-1812), the Rothschild family first prospered by lending to individuals and businesses but found it was more profitable to engage with governments. They create demand by instigating wars, financial panics, revolutions, famines, pandemics, and depressions while hiding their identity. Europeans have named the Rothschild's "The Merchants of Death" or sometimes "The Brotherhood of Death." Like the Wizard in the *Wizard of Oz*, they hide behind a screen while masterminding events. The play "*Marmion*" by Sir Walter Scott describes modern-day banking *"Oh what a tangled web we weave, when first we practice to deceive."*

The Federal Reserve's primary objective is to control events. *"Permit me to issue and control a nation's money, and I care not who makes its laws!"* is a famous quote by Mayer Amschel Rothschild. *The Lords of Finance - The Bankers Who Broke the World* by Liaquat Ahamed exposes banking tyranny. Then there is Carroll Quigley's book *Tragedy and Hope - A History of the World in our Time*. On page 324 (out of 1348 pages!), Quigley writes:

> *"In addition to these pragmatic goals, the powers of financial capitalism had another far-reaching aim, nothing less than to create a world system of financial control in private hands able to dominate the political system of each country and the economy of the world as a whole..."*

CITY OF LONDON

The term "The City of London" was initially identified by Lyndon LaRouche. His ideas and organization supercedes his death by the Schiller Institute, founded by Helga Zepp-LaRouche. This modern-day British Empire consists of interlocking political and corporate cartels that wages war to pursue power and control.

The City of London is a global financial center made up of former insignificant outposts of the British Empire, such as the Cayman Islands, the British Virgin Islands, and Bermuda. These offshore jurisdictions capture wealth from across the globe and funnel it to the City where the rich and powerful hide their assets from the tax collector. The City is a semi-autonomous state within a state, a financial district, and the beating heart of the global hub of tax haven activity. It has its representative in parliament who has special privileges, and the mayor's primary duty is to serve as an ambassador for the United Kingdom's financial services. London has two mayors, one presides over the greater London, but he has no jurisdiction over the square mile that makes up the City of London. The City never has to declare assets to the British government because it is an ancient, autonomous city established under the Roman Empire. It has a mayor, independent laws, and parliament has no authority over it; financiers control the politics. Global companies vote in British elections via the City of London, and the City's lobbyist wields the most power in parliament, where it has controlled politics for more than 800 years. When member corporations face financial difficulties, they receive bailouts from the British government where money flows from the middle class to the rich.

The author Nicholas Shaxson in his book *Treasure Island* uncovers how offshore tax evasions have cost the US taxpayer 100 billion dollars in lost revenue each year while bankers and multinational corporations operate side by side with nefarious tax evaders, organized criminals, and the world's wealthiest citizens. *Treasure Islands* exposes the culprits and its victims and shows how the elite route one-half the world's trade through tax havens. Politicians are spokespersons of the financial elite, such as Goldman Sachs. Simultaneously, the elite funnel twenty-five percent of international finance through the City of London and its offshore British territories, which make up the second British empire.

The City of London uses the fiat money system as leverage in their goal of world domination, a one-world government, a banker's dictatorship. Sovereign nations, especially the US, China, and Russia, must hold a summit to ban together to come against the City of London, the merchants of death, to prevent its world domination. The City of London threatens Russia and China. Russia and China are not aggressive, and they do not seek world domination, but they are like a wasp nest. Left undisturbed, they do not pose a threat, but wasps can become a real danger if you hit the nest with a baseball bat.

BAIL-INS

The financial crises of 2008 ushered in the term "too big to fail," which regulators and politicians used to describe the rationale for rescuing some of the country's largest financial institutions with taxpayer-funded bailouts. Congress then passed the Dodd-Frank Wall Street Reform and Consumer Act of January 2010, which eliminated the option of bank bailouts but opened the door to bank bail-ins. In a bailout, the government makes creditors whole by using taxpayers' money. A bail-in allows big banks to confiscate creditors (depositors) savings. Fiat money is subject to politics, and politics can seize our money. Bail-ins institutionalized the concept of too big to fail since banks could be rescued by expropriating creditors' funds. Most EU countries, the UK, the US, Canada, Australia, and New Zealand, have plans for bail-ins.

It is unlikely that a bank would take all of our savings—but a partial confiscation could happen. Dodd-Frank gave banks the right to confiscate our money when bankruptcy threatens, but only deposits above the Federal Deposit Insurance Corporation (FDIC) for each account, which is currently $250,000. $250,000 is a lot of money for an individual, but not so much for a business owner. When you deposit money in a bank, you are an unsecured creditor. The Bank of International Settlements in Basel, Switzerland, the central bank for central banks, has sanctioned bail-ins. Banks in Argentina and Cyprus have confiscated depositor's money because their liabilities exceeded the country's GDP; consequently, large depositors faced a 40% levy rescuing the banks from collapse. In her book *Banking on the People in the Digital Age*, Ellen Brown explains how the new G-20 rules will usher in bail-ins for depositors.

When gold or silver gave the dollar value, we were protected, life had value, but we became naked when Congress severed the tie between gold and money, and the dollar became only the ghost of real money. In a fiat money system (fiat means "let it be" in Latin), life loses value because created money can finance wars; life is cheap. On August 15, 1971, President Richard Nixon told a national television audience that the government would no longer exchange gold for dollars from other countries. He then convinced the Fed to increase the money supply. Consequently, inflation in the 1970s averaged ten percent, and the prime interest rate hit a high of 21 percent in 1979. If it had not been for Paul Volcker, chairman of the Federal Reserve from 1979 to 1987, putting the brakes on the money supply, inflation, and interest rates would have continued to increase. The national debt was under a trillion dollars in 1979; today, it is approaching thirty trillion dollars! Today we are in a crack up boom. Ludwig von Mises postulated that in the face of excessive credit expansion, money will eventually become worthless leading to a crash in the economy.

Russia is the third-largest gold producer in the world after China and Australia. Gold gives the owner the ability to value hard assets, like labor, essential to a sound economy. While Russia and China are the world's largest creditor nations, America is the world's largest debtor nation. While Russia and China accumulate gold, America accrues debt. According to Standard and Poor's, near forty percent of its top 500 companies have a negative book value compared to fifteen percent in the 1980s. Negative book value means that if we sold off the company's assets, there would not be enough money to pay its debts. Cash infusions and government policies sustain zombie companies, giving the appearance of life as they crowd out viable businesses. Eventually, the economy will have to reset itself, and a gold stock provides the collateral to reboot the system.

RED QUEEN SYNDROME

To keep production up, the number of oil wells will have to continue to increase. Economists call this phenomenon "The Red Queen Syndrome," which alludes to the character in *Alice in Wonderland*, who famously declared that she had to run faster and faster to stay in the same place. The federal government is caught in a Red Queen Syndrome because it spends more money from debt than taxation. Because of interest, it has to pay more to stay in the same place.

We have borrowed against the future and stuck the young generation with debt. Artificially low interest rates were a shot in the arm to a rising stock market as people sought higher returns, but the Fed has been injecting money into a corpse. Still, the market gives false signals as stock prices are no longer a function of the real economy. Debt is growing faster than growth in most of the world, but especially in the United States. The rapidly increasing deficit from year to year is not sustainable because corporations must refinance the debt. The easy money policies of the Federal Reserve will eventually crash the market while making fewer choices for the average stock buyer as corporations acquire their stock with cheap money.

Credit agencies have issued a world debt downgrade warning due to deepening global uncertainty and risks. According to the Institute of International Finance, world debt exceeds 260 trillion dollars, which is three times the size of the world economy. Moody fears that we are in a debt trap because the Federal Reserve keeps creating money to rescue the plutocrats at the expense of everyone else. A plutocracy is a system ruled by persons of power and influence.

The one thing that everyone understands is that the game ends when indebtedness exceeds our ability to finance the debt. When the government borrows money to fund social security, unemployment insurance, food stamps, Medicare, and Medicaid, the system will implode. People will either accept their poverty or rebel. As the spread between income classes increases, as the middle falls out of the middle class, we experience strife. But will this lead to violence? It is not a lack of courage that prevents rebellions as much as indifference. Indifference trumps cowardice. It's not fear that keeps people in check; it's acceptance. There is no need to fight tyranny actively; all we need to do is refuse our consent; we must choose not to participate. A good book on the subject is *The Politics of Obedience - The Discourse of Voluntary Servitude* by Étienne de la Boétie, 1552, reprinted by the Mises Institute 2015.

After the government funds its mandatory programs, Congress cannot support the military or federal employees without borrowing money. Currently, the US debt is higher than the world's gross domestic product. To balance the budget, Congress would have to raise taxes by at least fifty percent or eliminate the federal government. If Congress cuts entitlements and pensions, people will riot in the streets.

The US government lost its triple-A rating for the first time in 2011 because of its prolific spending and borrowing. A bankrupt government cannot prosper its citizens. Money creation is the toxic waste from the rear end of a central bank system that consumes fraud. According to the International Monetary Fund (IMF) of the United Nations, the world faces a black hole of debt.

The artificially low interest rates are trashing the investment portfolios of pension funds robbing the middle class of a secure future, leaving society vulnerable to increased interest rates. Loan delinquencies are spiking, and student debt now exceeds 1.6 trillion dollars. An indentured servant was a person who came to America under contract to work for someone who financed his passage until he paid the debt. Today's college students are indentured servants because the government enticed them with generous loans and then saddled them with years of debt that they cannot erase through bankruptcy. When politicians encourage students to bury themselves in debt, they play a script from Saul Alinsky's *Rules for Radicals*. In his book *How to Create a Socialist State*, Alinsky advocates a debt-ridden society, control of the educational system, and a gross uneven distribution of wealth as a means to change the culture.

An increase in debt can lead to an economic upswing, but it can also deepen a recession. The low interest rates encouraged people to chase after higher returns, thus the rising stock market. But what happens when the market heads south? Corporations could have taken advantage of the low rates by investing in goods and services, which some did. Still, too many embarked on creative financing to raise their share value in the stock market, bringing us into an age of phantom money, speculation, and market distortions. We are in trouble when too many companies make money on money instead of selling goods and services.

Low-interest rates mean that time has little value, and negative rates mean that time has a negative value. The financial world needs market rates to give time value. If money has an artificially low return rate, then we have gone down the rabbit hole; we have sunk into a house of mirrors where nothing makes sense. We exist in an *Alice in Wonderland* world; we have gone through the Looking Glass where investors make money on the appearance of growth, but not growth itself. When corporations buy their stock to raise the market price, they profit from the shadow of growth. When the Federal Reserve creates money to purchase stock and government debt, it creates an illusion of prosperity, but not prosperity itself. And when the government injects trillions of new dollars into the economy, it blows air into a false economy.

FALSE PRICE SIGNALS

GE used to be one of America's biggest companies; now, it has the world's biggest pension fund black hole. From 2008 to 2017, GE's executives borrowed almost 40 billion dollars from its pension fund. This stock buyback makes it look like earnings are increasing while revenues stagnate.

Airlines spent a vast portion of their government money on share repurchases instead of investing in infrastructure, research, and development. According to the *Financial Times*, CEO Doug Parker of American Airlines made $150 million selling its stock from 2013 and 2020. Executives like Parker engineer higher stock prices to earn generous compensations while cannibalizing corporate balance sheets, leaving us on the hook for government bailouts when the company fails. These stock buybacks distort valuations by inflating bubbles while enabling these ghouls of deception to commit the most massive corporate plunder in history as false price signals mitigate a false economy.

When wealth destruction overpowers wealth creation, we live in an Alice in Wonderland world. For example, Goldman-Sachs does not invest; it manipulates, orchestrates, and plunders, leading to a financial return for Goldman, but asset destruction for everyone else. For instance, it sells junk bonds to Iceland by deceiving them into believing that the bonds will yield a positive return. Goldman gains from the deception by betting in the derivatives market (it buys a credit default swap) that the bonds will fail. Thus, its client will lose, and Goldman will gain because it has rigged the system in its favor.

Goldman-Sachs, JP Morgan, and others use a sleight of hand with clients, such as a pension fund. A trader makes a highly speculative trade, but he does not account for that trade, only the street name. The trader then waits several days, and if the transaction is profitable, he supplies the account number to the corporation's super wealthiest clients. If the trade ends up as a loss, the trader provides a pension fund's account number. Stockbrokers call this deception "parking a trade" or a "look back call trade." These trades are illegal, but the mechanics of regulatory oversight are so opaque to be meaningless. These trades enable JP Morgan Bank and other ghouls of deception to profit by separating risk from reward.

CANTILLON EFFECT

Richard Cantillon was a French Irish economist in the 18th century who wrote about money. The Cantillon Effect recognizes that the people who own the most assets benefit first from low-interest rates, and indebted people benefit the least. Whereas the wealthy invest the money, the low interest encourages the poor to borrow. Persons who profit the most from money creation can access the cash at the beginning, such as the federal government, wealthy individuals, corporations, and big banks. The Cantillon Effect causes a redistribution of income from the middle class to the rich, enabling a class of cantillonairs. The ghouls of financialization have made us victims of low interest rates leading to economic vandalism, causing a fraud cycle. We have become workers on a multinational plantation living in a two-tier economy. America is one nation with two systems.

As the inequality of income increases, a vicious cycle takes hold with the elite favoring their own. The rich and powerful look at us differently than they do one another. The elite believes that we are to serve them because they are a higher form of humanity. The super-rich are invisible to the rest of us; they can travel anywhere in the world, stay at expensive hotels, eat at exclusive restaurants, and always associate with the same people.

This growing inequality is a worldwide phenomenon; it is happening in China, Russia, India, France, Canada, even in social democracies like Finland, Sweden, and Germany. People have taken to the streets in Chile, demanding the government address economic inequality. A good book on the subject is *Plutocrats - The Rise of the*

New Global Super-Rich and the Fall of Everyone Else by Chrystia Freeland. French economist Thomas Piketty explains in his 700-page book *Capital* that wealth concentrated in fewer hands will lead to riots. This concentration of wealth empowers the rich, enslaves the middle class, and destroys the free market. Piketty believes that we are on the road to patrimonial capitalism, whereby all power stems from a group of elite leaders.

DEMISE OF THE MIDDLE CLASS

Tom is a member of the middle-class. Having been married to June at an early age, life has been difficult raising three children. June's job as a teacher has enabled them to pay the interest on their Visa bill each month, the rent, and the monthly payments on their two cars. Not being able to get decent interest on their retirement money, they invested in the stock market. As long as they remain healthy and nothing unexpected happens, they can make it from payday to payday. But a downswing in the stock market, the loss of a job, an increase in the price of food, or unexpected doctor bills, will throw the family into a crisis.

The middle class is postponing retirement, making them the fastest-growing group of workers. There has been a sharp increase in suicides for people between 55 and 65 because of healthcare costs. If you are 64, you might die of a disease, but Medicare covers you if you are 65 and older. So far, this house of cards has been kept afloat by personal and public debt and a strong dollar on the world market—but debt is rising, and the dollar is falling.

BRICS is an acronym for Brazil, Russia, India, and South Africa. The BRICS countries account for 40 percent of the world's population and about 20 percent of the world's domestic product. The BRICS are considering abandoning the dollar and using a gold platform when trading amongst one another. This new gold standard is a step to end the US dollar's domination. When this happens,

America's influence in the world will shrink even further as it loses its international transactions position. As more countries sell off their US securities for gold, the geopolitical tectonic will continue to shift away from America. China now dominates the world economy while replacing the US as the world's economic powerhouse.

AMERICA'S EXCEPTIONALISM

Most Americans have fallen victim to the belief in American exceptionalism. In their minds, America is not just big and powerful—but an exception to all others. Countries have risen and fallen throughout history, but America is a nation blessed by God and set apart. They believe that America is the bearer of freedom and liberty, and Americans are morally superior to all other people and all other nations. This belief in American exceptionalism has justified America's military exploits and has become a psychological barrier blinding Americans to geopolitical facts.

Germany's unification of East and West in 1990 could have been the start of economic cooperation between Russia, Europe, the United States, and, eventually, China. But the window of opportunity was closed when America declared itself the only superpower and adopted a policy of controlling the world by military and economic warfare. Once America viewed European countries as allies, it now treats them as underlings and considers cooperation between Europe and Russia as a threat to US dominance.

Russia's Gazprom and Europe's big energy corporations have joined forces to build a second gas pipeline, Nord Stream 2, beneath the Baltic Sea, connecting Russia and Germany and, eventually, Europe. Not only would Nord Stream 2 preclude the necessity of expensive US liquefied natural gas (LNG) from being imported by the EU, it would make Europe and Russia partners with a real incentive to remain on good terms. Such a geopolitical turn of events has all the potential to render NATO obsolete.

The US has placed harsh sanctions on contractors and even target insurance and certification companies working with Russian vessels to complete the project. Swiss-Dutch construction company Allseas was intimidated into suspending its operations on the pipeline due to US pressure, and Ukraine and Poland have sided with Washington opposing the pipeline.

A White Paper is an informational document highlighting a complex issue. In a White Paper leaked to the *New York Times* shortly after the Soviet Union's collapse in 1991, Paul Wolfowitz, an American diplomat and former President of the World Bank, exposed Washington's true intentions. According to the White Paper, the US did not intend to have a peace dividend. It did not plan on spending the money saved on healthcare, infrastructure, affordable housing, helping the poor, or improving the educational system. But instead, Washington funded covert operations, making it clear that the US must dominate all others in a zero-sum game, whereby someone wins, and someone loses. It's like Toby Keith's song - *Courtesy of the Red White and Blue* - *"And you will be sorry that you messed with the US of A cause we'll put a boot in your ass it's the American way."*

FAR EAST

Russia's largest liquid natural gas producer (LNG) is upgrading its facilities in the Far East, and Russia's gas giant Gazprom is working on completing a pipeline to China. Russia has signed a preliminary agreement with Japan's Saibu Gas under which the companies will cooperate in gas delivery to the Asian-Pacific market. France is a partner with Russia in at least one gas LNG project. Italy wants to partner with Russia to build a gas plant in the Russian Arctic despite the US sanctions. These events reveal how confusing things can get because one of the Italian gas companies involved is Nuovo Pignone which is owned by General Electric. An Italian and a Turkish company signed a contract worth $2.2 billion for an LNG platform construction. To avoid US sanctions, Russia's largest privately-owned natural gas producer, Novatek, has managed to avoid American penalties by switching its financing from dollars to Euros and has won $12 billion worth of Chinese funding to replace Western money.

The European Union is considering switching payments from the US dollar to the euro after Washington threatened European firms working in Iran. Iran now uses the Chinese yuan in its bilateral trade with China and the euro when trading with European countries and the ruble and rial with Russia. Venezuela has also abandoned the dollar and has begun using the yuan. China has pulled off a huge 'diplomatic coup' by finalizing the world's largest free trade agreement, the Regional Comprehensive Economic Partnership (RCEP), which incorporates 15 Asia Pacific countries representing a third of the global economy. Japan may expand a major regional free trade pact to include China. Asia Pacific countries ignored the US as they cooperated in the world's largest trade deal. Known as the Comprehensive and Progressive Agreement for Trans-Pacific Partnership (CPTPP), the accord includes 11 countries in the Asia-Pacific that decided to keep their markets open after the US switched to protectionist policies.

EAST vs. WEST

China makes its products, and it makes our products. In March of 2000, President Bill Clinton supported China as a member of the World Trade Organization (WTO) because he believed China would import more US products and import American values, including democracy. But Clinton did not understand the Asian world and its thousand-year civilization.

Robert Lighthizer, the US trade representative in the 1990s and a former trade negotiator with China, stated that if the WTO admits China, it will become a dominant nation, and no manufacturing job in America would be safe. America has finally recognized the right problem but has embarked on the wrong solution. Instead of waging a trade war and weaponizing the dollar, America should encourage saving and investing. According to the National Interest Security Company's figures, America can only build two submarines a year. Still, it has to retire three a year because of the trade war with China. In some cases, the military only has one supplier, and that supplier is China.

The one rare earth mine operating in the United States sends its ore to China for processing, but it faces a 25% import tariff imposed by China. As the trade war escalates, China has threatened to block rare earth metals vital to technology, electric cars, clean energy, and defense. About 35% of global reserves are in China, the most globally, and the country is a mining machine, producing 70% of total rare earths in 2018. One reason Elon Musk is building a factory to build his electric cars in China because he needs the rare earth metals for his batteries.

While America funds sports stadiums, China builds ship factories; while America lags in 5-G technology; China is developing 6-G technologies and makes high-speed rail and electrical charging stations throughout the country. The US used to produce 25 percent of the world's semiconductors; now, it provides only five percent. China has spent 11 billion dollars on a quantum computing center, while America has spent one billion dollars. America rewards executives according to their stock price. China rewards executives according to the company's economic success. China is cracking down on big tech companies that bundle financial services for consumers because it is concerned about the concentration of power among a few big companies. At the same time, America has done nothing to stem the growth and influence of American high-tech companies. Americans tend to be short-term thinkers; China develops long-term plans. The Chinese are busy buying US real-estate and companies, while America remains more parochial, except for military bases.

When America first shipped its manufacturing to China, the idea was that China would do low value-added jobs, and America would innovate. Still, America has put too much into the social, environmental, and military sectors and not enough in research and development. When a country loses its innovation on the factory floor, it loses innovation at the top.

Only two American banks are in the top ten globally, and for the first time, China has replaced the US with the most companies on the Fortune 500 Global List. The United States maintains nearly 800 military bases in more than 70 countries and territories abroad; China has only one installation to support. Whereas America spends on defense, China builds infrastructure. Economically China is not a communist country. In a communist country, government planning replaces the price mechanism. In China, people can own a business and make a profit. Market forces determine the decisions of what to produce and what price to charge. However, China's political system is centralized.

More than one hundred of the world's largest companies have their headquarters in China. According to Credit Suisse, a leading financial services company in Switzerland, China has overtaken the US in terms of its wealthiest people because the profit motive is alive and well. Because entrepreneurship is strong, China is in an upswing economically while America is headed south. Americans are good at creative financing, at buying back their company's stock to raise the value, at buying and then cannibalizing other companies—but the system is not as good at improving the real economy as in China.

It appeared that much of the world would join America in its quest for a new world order twenty-five years ago, but today, countries are more independent. It is an illusion that countries that modernize will also westernize. Jim Rogers, a billionaire and co-founder of the Quantum Fund and Soros Management Fund, moved his family to Singapore from the United States because he wanted his daughters to learn how to speak Mandarin. He believes that, in the future, anyone who cannot address themselves in the Chinese language will not be able to compete.

The West has nation-states, but China is a civilization disguised as a country. The Chinese customs, their sense of family, and social relationships stem from Confucian values. China is hugely diverse and pluralistic and decentralized in many ways because Beijing cannot control a civilization of 1.3 billion people. Unity is most important for the Chinese; the government maintains the Chinese culture. Whereas most countries, especially the US, consider themselves to be multiracial, the Chinese share a cultural identity.

In the East, the relationship between the state and the individual is very different than that in the West. In Western cultures, the authority of the state is a function of democracy. The Chinese government enjoys more legitimacy and moral authority without being a democracy because it is the guardian of Chinese civilization. Whereas the West has always experienced conflicts, the Chinese state has been supreme with no serious rivals for over a thousand years. Westerners believe that the state's powers need to be defined and constrained—the government is the family's patriarch in China.

China may be more restrictive than the West in terms of personal freedoms, such as freedom of religion, freedom of the press, the right to bear arms, and experimenting with a point system that monitors all citizens. Still, these are social and political differences, not economic differences. China's ruling party is the Communist Party, but this is a title, not a system.

If you consider China from only a Western perspective, you do not understand China. For the past 200 years, the West has so dominated world events that Westerners believe it is unnecessary to understand non-Western cultures. This arrogance, this short-sightedness, could be the downfall of Western civilization. Because the East has had to learn from the West, the East is more cosmopolitan than the West. The East is far more knowledgeable about the West than the West is about the East. In the emerging world, the East, economic policy has been more orthodox, their situation more stable, and their balance sheets stronger. The East is not immune to declining economic conditions, but the West sits on a cliff edge.

CHAPTER 7

VASSALS AND ENEMIES

*G*eneral Electric's earliest products were incandescent light bulbs, electric locomotives, x-ray machines, electric stoves, and laser light technology before expanding into the financial sector under Jack Welch's leadership. Between 1981 and 2001, Welch increased the company's book value by eliminating personnel expertise, technology, and manufacturing. By the time he stepped down in 2001, he had transformed the company from a $25 billion manufacturing company into a $130 billion financial conglomerate. But because so much of GE's business was in the financial sector, its stock plunged 42 percent in 2008. Warren Buffett saved the company from bankruptcy by investing three billion dollars. On June 19, 2018, GE's more than 100-year run on the Dow Jones Industrial Average came to an end.

Key people left GE and became executives at other corporations, where they transformed them into financial institutions. David Calhoun, a protégée of Jack Welch, assumed the presidency of Boeing Aircraft. Under Calhoun, the company took advantage of the low interest rates and spent four billion dollars on stock buybacks in his attempt to become a leader in financial engineering instead of aircraft engineering. After blowing forty-three billion dollars on share-buybacks in six years, Boeing had to borrow ten billion dollars to stay afloat on top of a 9.5 billion dollar credit line. Watch for a change in the term "stock buyback" to "earnings enhancement."

Authorities used to consider executives buying back their company's stock to raise the price for personal gain insider trading, but this is no longer the case since 1982 when President Ronald Reagan made it legal. Turning the company into a financial institution is a factor that led to the 747 Max Aircraft disasters in 2019. From 2016 to 2017, Boeing fired 8,000 employees, including 1,332 engineers, and hired subcontractors overseas who were cheaper than full-time American engineers. Even though Boeing has reported its first loss in twenty years and its liabilities exceed its assets, its stock price tends to increase because investors know that their friends and partners in Congress will rescue the company if necessary.

Lockheed Martin has a high debt to equity ratio, where its executives have been wolves in sheep clothing. The government has spent 400 billion dollars on the F-35 fighter jet—but the plane cannot hit targets, and the aircraft has 800 plus software glitches and other flaws, according to a Pentagon review. Despite these flaws, Congress continues to shovel billions into the company. Bailouts are like Christianity without hell. Kleptocrats, a person who seeks personal gain at the expense of the governed, have transformed a viable economic system into a system that only benefits the rich and powerful, the oligarchy.

PRIVATE EQUITY

The oligarchy has transferred risk onto the balance sheets of pension funds, such as Calpers of California, the world's largest public pension fund, making them toxic waste dumps. Some pension fund managers are guilty of fraud by accepting junk bonds from investment banks and hedge funds. Others have taken low-grade bonds because they were lied to by the sellers, such as Goldman Sachs and Citadel Investment Group. Ken Griffin, the Citadel founder, paid 238 million dollars for a penthouse condominium overlooking Manhattan's Central Park. When pension funds try to sell their junk bonds, they are worth a lot less than the bankers told them.

Jamie Diamond, a billionaire and chairman of JP Morgan Bank, says he is against socialism. Yet, the government will save him when the economy tanks because his bank is too big to fail. When Donald Trump was President he was against socialism, yet he was willing to spend billions bailing out the airlines in return for partial ownership. While Boeing has a junk credit rating score, it can borrow from banks and the government. Yet JP Morgan makes it difficult for the average person to qualify for a mortgage by raising borrowing standards to a 20 percent down payment and a credit rating of at least 700. When JP Morgan or Boeing need help, the government showers them with money. When the homeowner falls too far behind on his mortgage, the lender evicts him. When big banks and favored institutions borrow money, they pay no interest or even negative interest, while everyone else pays a lot more.

We are putting our resources into the shadow of wealth instead of wealth itself. In the first three months of COVID-19, the US Treasury borrowed three trillion dollars from the Federal Reserve, which increased the national debt to 26 trillion dollars. And where did the bulk of this three trillion dollars go? It went into the banks' coffers because the US has no existing public infrastructure to get money to struggling businesses.

Since the 1930s, laws have restricted the federal government's activities and the Federal Reserve to the financial sector, but this is no longer the case. In March of 2020, Congress gave the Secretary of the Treasury the authority to make loans to eligible businesses, states, and municipalities. When Congress enacted the CARES Act in March of that year, it included half a trillion dollars for the Federal Reserve to support private lending and credit creation. Even though the law limits the Fed to the financial market, the Fed can circumvent the law by establishing special purpose entities (SPVs) that act as independent companies to make corporate purchases through BlackRock. Now, we have a partnership between the US Treasury, the Fed, and BlackRock, which, according to Max Keiser, host of the Keiser Report, the Fed owns about 30 percent of GDP. This partnership of the world's bankers and the US Treasury is replacing free-market vibrancy while allowing the Fed to acquire a larger slice of the economic pie. The Fed's acquiring an ever-larger share of the economic pie is an example of a prediction by Frédéric Bastiat, a French economist of the 1800s who once stated: *"When plunder becomes a way of life for a group of men in a society, over the course of time they create for themselves a legal system that authorizes it and a moral code that glorifies it."*

The Federal Reserve is now buying junk bonds from companies in Chapter 11 bankruptcy. Hertz Global Holdings, the rent a car company with a negative two billion dollars in equity, filed for bankruptcy in April of 2020, prompting the Fed to purchase $1.8 billion worth of Hertz bonds. Hertz's stock price increased tenfold after the filing, with one billion dollars' value of shares sold to BlackRock. Ditto for Whiting Petroleum, Pier 1, J.C. Penney, California Resources, and Chesapeake Energy saw their shares increase by at least seventy percent after declaring bankruptcy.

The Fed has plundered the future by lowering its reserve requirement to zero! The reserve requirement stipulates how much money banks must keep in their vaults as a cushion against withdrawals. When the Fed decreases the reserve requirement, it allows banks to lend more money while keeping less cash. This ratio was north of 20 percent through most of the Fed's first fifty years, including the Great Depression—but now it is zero, nada, nothing! We have entered an age of consequences where the Fed's kicking the can down the road has slammed into a dead-end, which is COVID-19. All empires end with massive debt and income inequality.

Adam Smith is well known for his book *An Inquiry into the Nature and Causes of the Wealth of Nations.* He describes how the invisible hand of self-interest and competition enables the free market to produce goods and services that consumers want at reasonable prices. His book *The Theory of Moral Sentiments* is less well known, where he argues that a free market system is dependent on a society with a solid moral fabric. It is not morally right for the system to favor one group over another; to have one set of rules for a selected group and another set of rules for everyone else, one set of rules for America and another set of rules for foreigners, and to have a gross uneven distribution of wealth.

VASSALS AND ENEMIES

Hegemony is the preponderant influence or authority over others. The world is rebelling against America's hegemony, America's sanctions and military threats. A sanction is a punitive or coercive measure or action that results from failure to comply with a law or rule. If a country fails to support American sanctions against purported enemies, the US can bar that person, that company, that country from the Federal Reserve Bank of New York, and can freeze their assets. Sanctions are an act of

war because they hurt, maim, kill the poor, the young, and the disadvantaged.

Russia has built two natural gas pipelines, Nord Stream 1 & 2, bringing gas from Russia to Germany and Europe, which poses a threat to America, so the US has threatened European countries with sanctions. Despite America's threats of sanctions, Germany insists that its robust economy requires a stable supply of natural gas, and Moscow is a suitable partner. The US has also threatened Germany with sanctions for trading with Iran, one of its major trading partners, no matter how big the financial hit.

When Washington pressures countries to buy US weapons and threaten countries who buy from Russia, it treats them as vassals. When the US pressures countries to buy American liquid gas instead of cheaper Russian gas, it makes enemies. When America sanctions European countries because they support the Nord Stream 2 Pipeline and the Turkish Pipeline, it treats them as underlings. When the US places sanctions against two International Court Officials for threatening to investigate America for war crimes in Afghanistan, it acts like a bully.

China depends on the South China Sea for its maritime trade routes. When the US places warships in the South China Sea, builds a military base close to China's border, and bans TikTok and Huawei from the American market without proof of wrongdoing, it treats China as an enemy and acting like a fascist state. Huawei has surpassed Samsung as the world's largest mobile phone vendor. But due to American restrictions, Huawei's primary supplier of advanced chipsets, manufactured by Taiwan Semiconductor Manufacturing, has stopped taking orders as it caved into US sanctions pressure.

US ALLIES PIVOT EAST

The North Atlantic Treaty Organization (NATO) is an intergovernmental military alliance between 29 North American and European countries. However, over the years, NATO has increasingly evolved from a purely defensive bloc into a "threat to international peace." NATO now serves the interests of Washington, along with its allies in London and Paris.

When the Cold War ended with the demise of the Soviet Union, authorities should have absolved NATO or at least changed its mission to a more peaceful one. It should have fostered a partnership with Russia. Instead, NATO chose the path of reviving old rivalries. To justify its existence, NATO needs an enemy, and the designated enemy is Russia and perhaps China. NATO's encroachment on the

Russian border is a threat to world peace. If NATO does not change its modus operandi, military conflicts could destroy Europe. At the same time, there are tensions within the G-7 nations of the United States, France, Canada, Japan, Germany, Italy, and England.

The proxy war in Syria is not a civil war; it is a conflict between Russia and the United States to control oil and a future gas pipeline. The South Pars/North Dome Gas Field is one of the world's largest gas fields, and Iran and Qatar share ownership of the field. The goal is to transport gas to Europe through Turkey. The conflict hinges on two proposals to get the gas to Turkey. The United States backs the plan to run the pipeline from Qatar through Saudi Arabia through Syria and Turkey. Russia supports the project that would run the pipeline from Iran through Iraq and Syria to Turkey. The Syrian conflict began when President Assad refused to permit the Qatar pipeline to go through his country. The US agreed with France, Qatar, Saudi Arabia, Turkey, and England in 2011 to replace President Assad with someone who would be agreeable to western goals. Because Russia has vast economic interests in Syria, Russia has defended Syria.

WORLD ORDER ONE, TWO, and THREE

World Order One emerged in World War Two's aftermath by establishing the World Bank, the International Monetary Fund, the United Nations, NATO, and later the European Union. The construction of the United Nations Building in New York City with money from David Rockefeller from 1946 to 1952 helped sustain the movement. World Order Two began around 1991 when the US won the cold war against Russia. But around 2007 and 2008, we entered World Order Three when the US started to lose its grip on world events.

But the times they are changing as alliances are shifting with nations claiming their independence from America and international rules and organizations like the European Union and NATO. International organizations are no longer serving their original mission, and the world is rebelling against American imperialism. Nations are turning inward as America's image as a world leader diminishes because countries wish to live by universal international laws and not be dictated by the US.

The word "order" does not mean "orderly" because we can have an unstable world order. A more accurate label for World Order 3 is World Disorder. World Order 1.0 is not coming back, and efforts to resurrect it will only slow the decline. If America continues to dominate world events, it will eventually find itself alone because it has relied on brute force instead of leadership. World Order 1.0 was a unipolar world with the United States as the leader. World Order 3.0 will be a multipolar world where nations share power. Whatever happens, Russia and China will play a pivotal role in shaping World Order 3.0. China may not have the ambition to rule the world, but it desires to rule Asia.

LUNATICS RUN THE INSANE ASYLUM

In the 2020s, we experience a comedy of errors, and lunatics are running the insane asylum. The 2007-2008 collapse is more a crime story than economics, and the same oligarchs are in charge. There has been no systematic response and no punishment for those who caused it. Since 2008 we have been in the eye of a financial hurricane due to money creation, debt, risky investments, and bailouts. We do not have a liquidity crisis; we have a solvency crisis that we cannot solve by creating money. Money creation has pulled from the future the wealth of the millennials and camouflaged the Fed's malfeasance.. We live in a world of holograms and phantom money.

Gosplan was the agency responsible for central planning for the USSR. Instead of a free market, Gosplan would set targets for prices and production regardless of the costs. The scheme collapsed because costs, what we pay to produce something, were often higher than prices, what we pay for the product. The Federal Reserve is America's Gosplan because it targets interest rates without considering the free market. The Fed is both an arsonist and a firefighter. Still, the system will not hold the Fed responsible for its wrongdoing as long as the government depends on it to keep insolvent companies afloat and to fund its debt.

The Federal Reserve has been the great facilitator in our race to the bottom because there is a massive disconnect between economic reality and monetary policies. In the middle ages, money lenders did their business on benches. Bankruptcy is an old Italian word from the 1500s that comes from the term "Banca Rotta," which means broken bench. When the banker could not pay his obligations, the people broke his bench. Our economic system is bankrupt, but there is no one to break its bench.

With escalating deficits and a national debt approaching 30 trillion dollars, the system has made us prisoners of debt while making interest the fastest-growing federal expense. A trillion is a million-million. One million seconds is four days, one billion seconds is 32 years, and one trillion seconds is 32,000 years! A trillion dollars in $100 bills would weigh 22 million pounds! Annual defense spending accounts for 15 percent of all federal spending, almost a trillion dollars, and roughly half of the government's discretionary spending. The national debt and military spending will absorb a larger share of the economic pie leaving less for social programs, the environment, education, law enforcement, and the infrastructure. Over 700 cash-strapped cities have halted plans to repair roads and upgrade water systems. Parts of California are already experiencing rolling blackouts. The US has 21 trillion dollars of unaccounted-for spending, nine trillion dollars of corporate debt, two trillion dollars in student loans, and trillions in unfunded liabilities. According to a US

Government Financial Report, the US has a negative $75 trillion net worth, about the same as the entire world economy!

What's even more worrisome than the national debt is the loss of America's Fiscal Constitution, a set of borrowing and budget rules first developed by Alexander Hamilton, America's first Treasury Secretary. Under the Hamiltonian System, the federal government should keep a surplus during prosperous times to meet challenges during slumps. But since the Great Depression of the 1930s, World War Two, and President Lyndon Johnson's two wars, Viet Nam and poverty, in the 1960s, we have moved away from Hamiltonian economics.

An excellent example of America's Fiscal Constitution loss is the student loan market. There has been a shortage of students making their student loan payments made worse by forbearance programs. Because so many students believe that the government will forgive their loans, existing loans are not getting paid down, while the market for new loans keeps increasing, and the balances continue to balloon. Economists call this situation a moral hazard. Moral hazard is the idea that a party protected in some way from risk will act differently than if they did not have that protection.

We would have experienced a collapse in the house of cards if it had not been for COVID-19 appearing in the nick of time to save the day. Just before the virus hit us, the world was on the verge of a financial crisis caused by rising interest rates. COVID-19 shut down business globally and therefore stalled the demand for money and postponed increasing interest rates. Debt and interest rates are in a fierce battle—they are enemies to one another. Debt can only grow in a world of low relative interest rates and positive expectations. An increase in real interest rates slows the economy and diminishes expectations. But, we have abolished the time value of money, and with negative rates only made possible money creation, the system has turned the clock backward.

Capitalism without capital is a zombie system, and we cannot have capital without savings. Economists define capital as the machines, tools, and buildings used to produce goods and services. Financial capital comes from savings used to generate capital. The US has been moving away from a capitalistic economy toward crony and financial capitalism. Crony capitalism has allowed preferential treatment for the well connected to take huge risks without fear of loss. Financial capitalism has allowed investors to make money on money; it has extracted equity from the system and left a debt carcass. Crony and financial capitalism encourage debt, rewards the rich, and punishes the saver, who is the bedrock of a free market system.

High finances is a Ponzi Scheme where the rich borrow from one another. Finally, no one has the money that backs up all the loans. These cash burn machines dominate the economy. America's Achilles's heel is short-term treasury bills that continuously mature at a time of rising interest rates. According to Guggenheim, an investment and asset management firm, asset price inflation caused by central banks' easy money policies is a Ponzi Scheme that will eventually collapse. According to Anne Walsh, Guggenheim's chief fixed-income chief, the Federal Reserve's easy money policies have created zombie companies that cannot survive a recession.

CHAPTER 8

MORE LIKE A PYTHON

*N*eoconservatives always need new dragons to slay, some sovereign who does not support them, or a leader to dethrone to be replaced by their puppet. Neocons view America as an empire and define the United States as the "indispensable and exceptional" country while convincing others to follow their lead. The neocons practice hegemony by dominating the policies of Washington, DC, and seek power and wealth by deception, unfair trade, gunboat diplomacy, and regime change wars, both domestically and internationally. When a president does not cooperate, they seek a change in administration because ideology holds sway over authority. Empires typically wield their hegemony by imposing order on the vanquished; neocons, however, seek hegemony by disorder, which never ends. In the Middle East and South America, we have had chaos and confusion brought on by America's regime-change wars. One need not look for a strategy here because geopolitics does not drive events—madness and schizophrenia cause events!

Here is how the neocons play the game. First, they fabricate a reason to accuse a country of some wrongful act. Second, they justify a regime change war, build military bases, impose sanctions, confiscate the county's resources, and employ terrorists to support their cause. Former Congresswoman Tulsi Gabbard introduced the Stop Arming Terrorist Act in 2016, which would prohibit the US government from funding and supplying weapons to AlQaeda, ISIL, and other terrorist groups. According to the National Priorities Project, the United States' cost to fund these terrorist groups is north of two trillion dollars. Gabbard claims that there is a covert strategy at work to keep the public in the dark concerning regime change wars and coup d'état.

LIKE A PYTHON

The US acts more like a python than a tiger—for example, it does not need Syrian oil, but controlling it deprives Syrians of heat in the winter. In gunboat diplomacy, the navy confiscated four Iranian vessels headed for Venezuela loaded with fuel and escorted them to an American port, thus depriving Iran of funds. The US threatens countries with sanctions if they do not support neoconservative' policies. Still, America's domination is experiencing death by a thousand cuts as much of the world is moving East, and the dollar is losing its status as the world's standard currency. The emergence of Russia, China, and India challenges America from above, and smaller nations are exiting America's dominance from below.

THUCYDIDES TRAP

There is a growing backlash from countries that see no future as America's indentured servants. We are experiencing de-globalization and de-dollarization as the rich hoard gold and the middle-class hoard toilet paper. We are in the grip of a Thucydides Trap, where the rising powers of Russia, China, and India are threatening to displace the American Empire. A Thucydides Trap occurs when the rise of a new power as a competitor to existing power results in political tensions and sometimes war. America's arrogance has led to foreign policies that have been clumsy and alienating while disregarding international etiquette. The more the US pressures the world to submit, the more nations will resist the pressure—pressure only works for a season.

Hegemony comes in many forms. In 2018, at the North Atlantic Treaty Organization (NATO) summit in Brussels, President Trump criticized Germany's chancellor, Angela Merkel, for supporting the Russian gas pipeline and demanded Germany buy American liquified natural gas for twice the price. The US has warned companies involved with the Nord Stream 2 pipeline to withdraw from the project, or the US would apply penalties according to Section 232 of the Countering America's Adversaries Through Sanctions Act (CAATSA). The US has demanded that NATO double its defense budget, or the US will withdraw its support. The US then deployed warships into the South China Sea and started building military fortifications near the Russian border.

Neoconservatives partner with companies such as Lockheed Martin, Boeing Aircraft, Raytheon, General Dynamics, and others. War is the most profitable industry, and neocons make consistent profits with constant wars while employing the "Madman Theory." The Madman Theory causes nations to view American leaders as irrational and volatile, thereby avoiding conflict for fear of an unpredictable response. Wesley Clark rose to the rank of four-star general and was named director for the Joint Chiefs of Staff's strategic plans and policy. A Pentagon senior official informed him two weeks after the Twin Towers incident that the military was plotting to overthrow Iraq, Syria, Lebanon, Libya, Somalia, Sudan, and Iran.

The 2019 film *Official Secrets* tells the story of how America pressured England into an illegal war. Katherine Gun was a British translator who worked for British intelligence. She lost her job after telling the *Observer Newspaper* how the US tried to spy with the intent to blackmail UN delegates to garner their support for a war against Iraq. Peter Henry Goldsmith was a British barrister and a former Attorney General for England. When America sought help to wage war against Iraq in 2002, Goldsmith advised Prime Minister Tony Blair that any war support would be illegal without a UN Security Council resolution. Blair agreed and opposed the war but then supported it after a trip to Washington DC. When Gun came to trial, the prosecution dropped all charges against her because the government did not want the trial to turn into a spectacle over the war's legality.

THE NEW AMERICAN CENTURY

The New American Century (PNAC) Project was a neoconservative think tank from 1997 to 2006. In a PNAC's policy document Rebuilding America's Defenses, the group called for total military world domination while waging multiple wars, particularly helping Israel. Many PNAC members, including Richard Perle and William Kristol, held high-level positions in the Reagan and Bush administrations. Long before the event of 9-11, the group postulated that should a catastrophic event take place, it would give America the excuse to pursue global hegemony.

The aim was to solidify America's worldwide power and convince the Defense Department to, 1) defend the homeland, 2) prepare to fight and win multiple wars simultaneously, 3) protect its superpower status 4) and transform the US defense department into a modern fighting force. They released their book *Present Dangers: Crises and Opportunity in American Foreign and Defense Policy in 2000*. The book is a collection of essays favoring the neoconservative worldview. It encourages the US to war against the seven countries they blamed for the Twin Towers' attacks, form a close tie with Israel, and encourage Israel to take a hard stand against the Palestinians.

During the 2003 Iraq invasion, several countries supported the US. But times are changing as countries are tired of America's hegemony, and fewer nations are willing to accept the official narrative, especially as it relates to Russia and China. By politicizing every issue and forcing countries to pick a side, there is a growing schism between America's words and deeds as the official statements often contradict the actual events. In October of 2020, when 39 countries sided with the US in the United Nations and issued a statement criticizing China over Xinjiang and Hong Kong, 70 countries issued a counter-statement defending China. Despite America's campaign to discredit Huawei, few nations have followed suit. When the US tries to convince Europe to eschew Russian gas, it receives little support. The more the US politicizes issues, the more pushback it will receive from the international community.

REGIME CHANGE WARS

According to the Watson Institute of International Affairs at Brown University, the US taxpayers' costs for the post-9-11 wars through the fiscal year 2020 is 6.4 trillion dollars. Verifiable war deaths since 9-11 are about 801,000, including 335,000 civilians. According to the American historian Christopher Kelly and British historian Stuart Laycock in their book *America Invades: How We've Invaded or Been Militarily Involved with Almost Every Country on Earth*, the United States has invaded or fought in 84 of the 193 countries recognized by the United Nations and has been militarily involved with 191 of 193 countries. But America's military exploits are coming to an end as America's influence is waning, its economy is faltering, and the dollar is sinking. As in all wars, it is a poor man's fight and a rich man's war.

Overthrow (2006) is a book by Stephen Kinzer, where he chronicles America's hegemony over fourteen countries, starting with Hawaii and ending with Iraq. Hawaii was an independent country before the United States overthrew its monarchy in 1893. He gives the history of how the United States toppled sovereign nations and replaced the democratically elected heads of state with a dictator who agreed to do America's bidding. *The Brothers*, another book by Kinzer, tells how John Foster Dulles and Allen Dulles were most responsible for America's hegemony and foreign conflicts described in *Overthrow*.

Mohammed Mosaddegh was Iran's first democratically elected Prime Minister in 1951. He was educated in America, loved everything American, and tried to westernize Iran. In 1952, his picture was on *Time's* cover when the magazine proclaimed him "man of the year." At the time, England controlled oil and railroads and kept the majority of the profits. When Mosaddegh tried to negotiate a better deal, England, with the help of the neocons in the CIA, sent Kermit Roosevelt, the grandson of President Theodore Roosevelt, to instigate a coup to overthrow him by way of lies, bribes, and deceit. The 1953 coup, named Operation Ajax, was successful and enabled England and America to restore power to the Shah. With the Shah's help, the US and Britain kept control of Iran's oil fields. The Shah ruled until 1979 when Grand Ayatollah Khomeini overthrew him in an Islamic revolution.

In April of 2018, 88 members of Congress sent President Trump a bipartisan letter stating that the US Constitution requires the President to seek Congressional approval before taking military action. The bombing and building of military bases in Syria, a country that poses no threat to America, is unconstitutional without congressional approval. If America had succeeded in toppling Syria's republic, Iran would have lost its only ally in the Middle East. Isolating Iran would be beneficial to America but especially helpful to Israel. The United States claims it can intervene anywhere in the world by coercion and, if the threats bear no fruit, by military intervention. The media often cloaks this intervention in national and world interest rhetoric and paints America as the world's policeman. But the real reason for the foreign exploits is to further neoconservative interests and increase the profits for American corporations, especially the defense industry, and enrich the world bankers.

MORALITY TRUMPS ECONOMICS

European standard of living is in decline, and violence is omnipresent because morality trumps economics. As Europe takes the moral high ground and bows to the false god of climate change, it is losing ground to the East. Eastern countries have priorities that stimulate growth, and the false religion of climate change does not grip them. The emerging world's economic and monetary policy is broadly orthodox. It is the West that is running an unorthodox monetary policy with quantitative easing. The financial crisis has turned into an economic crisis, and the economic situation is becoming more political. Europe depends on Russia for natural gas because its laws against fossil fuels and atomic energy have made natural gas the only viable fuel, and Russia has natural gas. The EU leadership in Brussels is in denial as events force Europe into Russia and China's arms as the center of gravity shifts.

Europe has lost ground to Russia, China, and India, as the European Investment Bank (EIB) adopted an unprecedented strategy to end fossil fuel energy projects. The European Union has a goal to become the world's first climate-neutral continent. The EIB has decided not to fund fossil fuel projects, including natural gas. These actions can only lead to an ever-lower standard of living for Europeans who will rebel when food becomes scarce and cannot heat their homes in winter or cool them in the summer. Seventeen hundred farmers drove their tractors to Paris, claiming that the high taxes needed to finance the Green Deal Projects drive them out of business. EU regulations are making them sacrificial lambs for environmental issues.

BLOWBACK

Because of rising tensions with Washington, many countries, including Russia, India, China, and Turkey, are seeking substitutes for the US dollar. Turkey's interests are moving East with an increase in imports of military hardware from Russia. Under Countering America's Adversaries Through Sanctions Act (CAATSA), passed in 2017, the US has to penalize countries who buy weapons systems from Russia. Despite the sanctions, according to *Business News*, foreign investments in Russia are expected to grow. Sanctions are short-sighted, and they will only weaken America's standing in the world.

The current US rhetoric against other countries and its disregard for moral standards has poisoned international relationships. America has alienated even its closest allies with America's first policies—rebellion is spreading. Even the Philippines suspended its military alliance with the US as it claims independence to conduct normal relations with China and neighboring states without American mediation. German and Irish voters have made it clear they want real change as recent elections have resulted in anti-American policies. Several Asian nations under Washington's tutelage may come to the same conclusion causing a domino effect as seismic political shifts move away from America are taking place throughout the western world.

PETRODOLLAR SYSTEM

World War II had a devastating effect on the global monetary system. A plan for restoring order came in 1944 at Bretton Woods, New Hampshire, when 730 delegates from 44 Allied nations met. Of paramount concern was replacing the British currency as the standard for settling international transactions. Because the United States held substantial gold reserves, the US dollar replaced the weakened British pound.

The Bretton Woods system linked the dollar to gold at a pre-determined rate of 35 dollars per ounce, while other countries pegged their currencies to so many ounces of gold. With countries pegging the value of their currencies to gold, each country knew relative values, which helped to facilitate international trade. Although the US agreed to pay in gold in exchange for dollars to other sovereign nations upon demand, this exchange was not a gold standard system. Because countries had confidence in the dollar, the dollar became the world's standard currency in international settlements. The system elevated the US dollar as demand shifted from the British pound to the US dollar.

America's inflation problem began in 1969 when President Richard Nixon inherited a recession from Lyndon Johnson, who had borrowed heavily, spent generously, and fought aggressively on the Vietnam War. Nixon imposed wage-price controls in 1971, ran budget deficits, and closed the gold window by reneging on the promise to exchange gold for dollars. These actions marked the end of the Bretton Woods System of dollars for gold and launched a freely flexible international exchange rate system.

The Bretton Woods system began to break down when countries experienced widely different levels of inflation. Congress was concerned that the abandonment of the "dollars for gold" arrangement could strike a blow to the dollar, and it sought a way to prop it up. The "Petro Dollar System" began when the Nixon Administration sent Henry Kissinger to Saudi Arabia in 1974 to convince the Saudis to accept only dollars for their oil. In exchange, Washington offered military assistance and protection for the region's oil fields. Instead of "dollars for gold," it became "dollars for oil," reestablishing the dollar as the world's standard currency.

Despite pressure from foreign nations to protect the dollar's value, Washington has spent beyond its means. Seeing that America is losing its grip on world events, witnessing the prolificacy of its spending and borrowing, the Saudis are anxious to establish friendlier relationships with its neighbors, threatening the Petrodollar System. Many countries distanced themselves from the dollar because blowback is in the wind as countries rebel against America's hubris. If people abandon the dollar, the Petrodollar system is caput.

THE QUICKENING

Countries are beginning to rebel against America's propaganda and wars as they see events overtaking the official narrative. Some people call this the Quickening; it is systemic and global. The center gives way when enough people realize that the official story has duped them, and they recognize that the rule of the fist has supplanted the rule of law. The neocon's dominance over world events, their global hegemonic power, began to give way with their failure to conquer Syria and Venezuela. These failures are watershed moments because the neocons could not destabilize the countries, marking the beginning of the end for the US proxy wars. Regional politics have shifted. Europe has become more dependent on Russia, and Russia has oriented itself closer to China and India. Neocons cannot succeed with their ad hoc responses to short-term pressures against the Russians and the Chinese's shared vision and efficiency. Sewing chaos and then taking advantage of the situation by going ever more into debt to finance sanctions and wars is a short-sighted policy.

The neocons require endless wars to stay in power-but they cannot invade other countries as freely as they did in Iraq in 2003, and they cannot violate international law as quickly. The world has changed as people realize that the false narrative has forced them into debt, has robbed them of their prosperity, and has moved the whole Eurasian economy towards the east. Constant war is profitable for the neocons, big banks, and some US corporations. War is not profitable for the common man and the nations devastated by war. Political capital is trust; without good leadership, the system falters, and people rebel.

A warfare state continually wages war against other countries for political and economic gain. The United States has placed sanctions against Cuba since 1962 when President Kennedy proclaimed a trade embargo. Sanctions tend to hurt the lower and middle-class the most—but not so much the upper class. America has weaponized commerce by imposing sanctions or embargoes against at least thirty countries and has put 400,000 people on a sanction list. The neocons have created enemies as an excuse for a record-breaking military budget and the riches that come with it. The Cold War with Russia came to an end in 1991, along with the Soviet Union. Without a giant to slay, the western powers should have dismantled NATO. Instead, the allies doubled down by fabricating the War on Terror.

Wars have left a vacuum that radical jihadists have filled that the US once supported but can no longer control. Major General Smedley is one of America's most decorated soldiers. In his 1935 book, *War is a Racket*, he describes war as *"where we measure profits in dollars and losses in lives and where the very few benefits at the expense of the very many."* The neoconservatives have controlled the narrative, but blowback is in the wind.

END OF NEOLIBERALISM

Neoliberalism emphasizes the value of free-market competition; it is a policy model that encompasses both politics and economics and seeks to transfer economic factors from the public sector to the private sector. Although there is considerable debate about the defining features of neoliberal thought and practice, it is most commonly associated with laissez-faire economics that favors free markets. Free markets are more efficient than centrally controlled economies, and free markets offer opportunities for freedom, entrepreneurship, and economic growth. Austrian economics recognizes that a free market system needs a stable central government to enforce fair rules. But neoliberal policies can lead to a concentration of power and wealth among the business elite while empowering the few and enslaving the many. In this neoliberal world, we went from high regulation to almost no limitation due to the Holder Doctrine. Eric Holder, the attorney general during the Obama Administration, declared that the government would not prosecute big banks for wrongdoing because they are systematically important.

Courts are lenient on millionaires who break the law encouraging fraud and collusion. We have a double standard with the wealthy getting a pass for white-collar crimes while the average person receives little mercy for low-level offenses. The burden of proof is different depending on the crime. Like cheating on taxes, the "I did not know" is no defense with low-level crimes. But with white-collar crimes, "*I did not know*" is a defense making the burden of proof different in these two cases. The government failed to prosecute corporate executives guilty of a crime, leading to 2007-2008, and then rewarded them for their transgressions.

Politics in America has said goodbye to first-class politicians or visionaries and has said hello to narcissists and moral lightweights who are more interested in self-service and less interested in public service. And if, by chance, the system presents us with an honest politician who has vision, the neocons entice or threaten him to do their bidding. President Trump campaigned on the promise of draining the swamp. Still, once in office, he appointed neocons from the financial sector, mostly Goldman Sachs, and generals who support the military-industrial complex. Since the 1950s, the military-industrial complex has dominated the federal government's discretionary spending.

During the 2007-2008 economic collapse, Henry Paulson, the Secretary of the Treasury and a past Chairman and Chief Executive Officer of Goldman Sachs, convinced Congress to bail out the big banks while offering no aid to small banks and the millions of victimized people who lost their homes. Neoliberalism has led to a concentration of power in banking, farming, social media, and other industries. Elitist policies cause a global revolt and frequent protests as people move to the left and right ideological extremes.

The government could have let the big banks fail in 2007-2008 because we have bankruptcy laws whereby a judge decides who gets what and how much while seeking new owners who will operate the business under a new set of rules. Bankruptcy avoids favoritism and moral hazard. When persons take huge risks because they know the government will protect them from losses, we have a plutocracy, rule of the few.

WESTLESSNESS

America is striving to maintain its global dominance economically and militarily. At the annual Munich Security Conference in Germany, world leaders disagreed over the relevance of the West. A chosen theme for the conference was "Westlessness," where participants questioned America's leadership. When the US secretary of state claimed that the West was winning over the East, his words fell on deaf ears. The West's hostility towards the East encourages an alliance between Russia, China, India, Turkey, and others. We are transitioning from a unipolar world dominated by the US to a multipolar world where nations share power.

Westlessness is what the West is doing to destroy itself. The West is fragmenting and becoming more divided while challenged by the East. The fault is not Russia or China—the responsibility lies within. Most of the world admires traditional western values, but western leaders and special interest groups commit political and cultural suicide. The concepts of nationalism and globalism have become blurred, and populist parties have risen to oppose neoliberalism.

CHAPTER 9

THE PUPPET MASTERS

*W*hat, or who is the deep state? Unelected people with authority comprise the deep state; they are politicians, bankers, executives of multinational corporations, and the military-industrial complex who may or may not contact one another. Presidents come and go, but agencies stay behind. A president only has the authority that his constituents give him. For example, let's say a president favors withdrawing troops from this or that country. But the military, the corporations who profit from war, and members of Congress prefer escalating war. Even though the president may have the legal authority to withdraw troops from combat, the deep state nullifies his jurisdiction. The Deep State seeks to control people and the world's resources; Even a sitting president depends on his advisors, who often have their agenda. The puppet masters of the deep state control the CIA, the Council of Foreign Relations, the military-industrial complex, the City of London, Wall Street, and the American Israeli Political Action Committee (AIPAC)—neoconservatives all.

The Deep State is a system behind the Shadow Government, including the Federal Reserve, the IMF, and the World Banking cabal. The Shadow Government is composed of secret intelligence agencies that use private contractors while binding them to secrecy under the threat of imprisonment, financial ruin, and personal harm. The system works against naysayers because it requires employees to sign the National Security Agency (NSA) and the Central Intelligence

Agency (CIA) secrecy agreements. The NSA can spy on our phones, laptops, Facebook, Skype, and chat rooms. This spying allows the NSA to build a "pattern of life" profile without a warrant if you are three contacts away from anyone it considers a potential threat to America. If you have 50 friends on Facebook, by the friend of a friend of a friend scenario, you have contact with over a million people. The CIA's counterpart is MI6; the Secret Intelligence Service is tasked mainly with covert overseas activities.

The Shadow Government controls the Central Intelligence Agency (CIA), the Trilateral Commission, and the Council of Foreign Relations (CFR). The CFR writes articles, and the State Department adopts the policies. Members of the CFR are in administrative positions, and its policies may not need Congressional approval. Former Judge Advocate General of the US Navy, Chester Ward, was a CFR member for twenty years and became one of its sharpest critics. Here is a quote from Admiral Ward:

> *"Once the ruling members of the CFR have decided that the US Government should adopt a particular policy, the very substantial research facilities of CFR are put to work to develop arguments, intellectual and emotional, to support the new policy, and to confound and discredit, intellectually and politically, any opposition."*

(Admiral Chester Ward, *Kissinger on the Couch*, pg. 144, 1975.)

The Shadow Government uses the State Department to benefit favored corporations. For example, if the US places sanctions on a country, it also threatens countries and corporations who do not cooperate. Propaganda tries to convince citizens that foreign interventions are patriotic and necessary to fight terrorism. Still, in reality, they enrich the world bankers, fund the military-industrial complex, support the shadow government, and fuel the fires of the deep state.

DARPA

DARPA is a part of the Deep State and is the wing of the US Defense Department that's responsible for developing technologies for military use. Annie Jacobson is an investigative journalist who was a 2016 Pulitzer Prize finalist and wrote about war, weapons, security, and government secrets. In her book *The Pentagon's Brain - An uncensored history of DARPA, America's Top Secret Military Research Agency*, she exposes how DARPA is responsible for innovations and inventions that have changed the course of wars. In 1958, Congress gave DARPA a mandate to develop weapons of mass destruction.

Initially, DARPA employed the Jason Scientists, a secret organization founded by Jason Goldberger. The Jason Scientists were level headed full-time professors and part-time DARPA employees. But when the Pentagon embraced the idea of autonomous weapons, such as hunter-killer drones controlled by artificial intelligence and other forms of robotic warfare, the Jason Scientists bulked. The Pentagon replaced them with the Defense Science Board. Full-time scientists sit on the boards of the major defense contractors such as Boeing, Lockheed, General Dynamics, and Raytheon—thus closing the loop between the government and the military-industrial complex.

The main driver in veterans' suicides is the moral injury that occurs when persons transgress against their belief system, against their fundamental values against their family, friends, and community while growing up. Acts committed against this personal belief system make a person believe he is not the person he wants to be or the person he thought he was. Military veterans make up eight percent of the adult population in America, yet they commit thirteen percent of adult suicides. Data from Veterans Affairs shows that suicides by soldiers sent to war in foreign lands are many times higher than stateside soldiers, and the number of soldier suicides exceeds the number killed in battle. The Department of Veterans Affairs released a report in 2017 showing that 60,000 veterans died of suicide between 2008 and 2017.

Starting with the War on Terror after 9-11, DARPA turned toward social engineering. For example, Narrative Networks is a program that researches the natural chemical oxytocin, which plays a role in social bonding; it is the brain's moral molecule. A breast-feeding mother, for example, emits oxytocin. Thus the military can inject oxytocin into its soldiers, making them a submissive fighting machine with no moral conscience. In January 2017, about 3,000 of the world's wealthiest people met in Davos, Switzerland, where they gather every year to discuss how they can rule the world. At this meeting, Bill Gates initiated a working group called the Coalition of Epidemic Preparedness (CEP). The CEP participants were the Gates Foundation, Norway, India, Japan, and Germany. Other participants were Oba and Moderna, two giant pharmaceutical companies, DARPA, and the US Army Medical Research Institute of Infectious Diseases.

GOVERNMENT WASTE

Dr. Mark Skidmore, a professor at Michigan State University and Catherine Austin, has researched the Department of Defense and the US Department of Housing and Urban Development funds and found $21 trillion in unaccounted transactions, almost as much as the national debt! This unaccounted-for spending violates the US Constitution. The Constitution states in Article 1, Section 9, Clause 7: *"No money shall be drawn from the treasury, but in consequence of appropriations made by law; and a regular statement and account of receipts and expenditures of all public money shall be published from time to time."*

The government's waste is so vast that a report from the Government Accountability Office stated that the Pentagon received 95,613 whistleblower alerts between 2013 and 2018. The report noted that the Pentagon has a standard operating procedure of merely making up numbers to balance the books. The armed services have no unified accounting system, and no one is privy to all the facts. At the end of every year, it creates reports based on invented numbers without proof of documentation. Congress passed a law in 1990 demanding annual audits of all government agencies; the Department of Defense finally submitted to an audit in 2018. After Congress spent $413 million and hired 1,200 auditors to access 21 Pentagon agencies, the auditors concluded that the Pentagon's books are inaudible.

The Office of Inspector General (OIG) gave a small group the responsibility to determine what parts of federal spending pose a national security issue. They put spending that they declare is a security threat in category B, and the rest they leave in category A. The OIG releases A, but it does not reveal B to the public. Formally federal expenditure was not transparent, but the law at least favored citizens.

CORPORATOCRACY

Corporatocracy is a term used to refer to an economic and political system controlled by corporations or corporate interests. The corporatocracy hires economic hitmen who convince countries to take out loans from the World Bank and the International Monetary Fund in hopes they will default. The coronavirus has opened a door for the IMF to extend loans to impoverished countries leading to more concessions and the IMF taking ever more control. Once a country is bankrupt, the IMF extracts trade-offs. For example, instead of paying its debts, a state will relinquish its mineral rights or hand over revenue from the country's airports. The IMF can force them to cut spending on retirement benefits and other social programs—the money saved goes to the central bankers. If these tactics fail, the neocons use intimidation, assassinations, and war to accomplish their goals.

Evo Morales is a former union leader who became Bolivia's first indigenous president, winning election in 2006. Although Morales had a 60 percent vote, within 48 hours, the Organization of American States (OAS) declared the election a fraud and placed Jeanine Áñez, a person sympathetic to Washington as the de facto president. Morales wrote on his Twitter that the coup against him was *"a political and economic conspiracy coming from the United States."* An excellent read on the subject is *The Confessions of an Economic Hit Man* by John Perkins.

THE WHISTLEBLOWERS

A whistleblower is a person who exposes secretive information or activity within a private or public organization that is deemed illegal, unethical, or not correct. The Espionage Act of 1917 and its amendment of 1918, and the Sedition Act, are perhaps the most controversial laws ever passed in the United States because they curtail the freedom of speech. The Espionage Act declared it unlawful for any person to publish information that the President claims to be helpful to the enemy. The Sedition Act made it illegal to *"utter, print, write, or publish any disloyal, profane, scurrilous, or abusive language about the form of government of the United States."*

June 2017 was the one-hundredth anniversary of the Espionage Act. To commemorate the centennial, President Trump suggested that the government should prosecute journalists who leak classified documents. Some of the defendants are whistleblowers of government waste, fraud, or abuse. The government can declare anything classified information and then prosecute people who divulge the information to the public.

Previously, the justice department made a distinction between government employees who leaked the information and the recipients of the data, giving the recipients first amendment protection. The Trump administration decided to prosecute the receiver and the giver, thus threatening every person who publishes information. The government has convicted fifty-two people under the Espionage Act. Nearly half of the convicted persons were whistleblowers exposing government crimes or people who were against the mainstream narrative. Authorities do not consider a person treasonous when the government condemns him under the Espionage Act. A person who commits treason is a person who wages war against the US or gives the enemy aid and comfort. The government has convicted 20 people for treason; half of them were broadcasters, journalists, and news correspondents accused of propagandizing the enemy.

While employed by the RAND Corporation, Daniel Ellsberg released the *Pentagon Papers* to *The New York Times* and other newspapers. Ellsberg's leak helped turn public opinion against the Vietnam War. When the government sought to prevent the newspaper from reporting on the *Pentagon Papers*, the newspaper fought back. The U.S. Supreme Court later determined that the newspapers were acting in the public interest.

Julian Assange is an Australian editor, publisher, and activist who founded WikiLeaks in 2006. WikiLeaks came to international attention in 2010 when it published a series of leaks provided by U.S. Army intelligence analyst Chelsea Manning. Wikileaks disclosed nearly 750,000 sensitive military and diplomatic documents revealing America's war crimes, human rights abuses, and corruption. The United States indicted Julian under the Espionage Act of 1917, and he was the first person to face persecution in the United States for publishing classified information. Assange and Manning's imprisonment is an attack on freedom of the press while protecting acts of imperialism.

Edward Joseph Snowden is an American whistleblower who copied and leaked highly classified information from the National

Security Agency (NSA) in 2013 when he was a Central Intelligence Agency employee. The documents provide a public window into the NSA and its international intelligence partners' secret mass surveillance programs, operating without any public oversight and outside the US Constitution's limits. The US government has charged Snowden with theft. He presently resides in Russia.

William Binney is a former intelligence official with the National Security Agency (NSA) and a whistleblower. He retired in 2001 after serving 30 plus years with the agency. He has been critical of the mass surveillance policies of Americans under George W. Bush and Barack Obama. Binney has revealed that the three-plus years of Russiagate was a witch hunt against Trump and was a manufactured hoax. Roger Stone is a political consultant who the neoconservatives persecuted for his role in the successful election of President Donald Trump in 2016. Another victim is Lyndon LaRouche, who authorities prosecuted because he irritated the Bush's by contradicting them in public. Robert Mueller, the same special counsel who spearheaded the Russiagate investigation against President Trump, was directly involved in the 1980's Department of Justice "Get LaRouche" campaign resulting in multiple trials and his 1989-1994 incarceration.

The Constitution guarantees Americans fundamental rights and freedoms. Tulsi Gabbard introduced bills in Congress that would protect whistleblowers and would reform the Espionage Act. If passed by Congress, the bills would drop all charges against Edward Snowden and Julian Assange. The bills never became law and Tulsi left Congress in 2020.

CHAPTER 10

WHAT A TANGLED WEB

*W*hen the *New York Times* published the Pentagon Papers in 1971 exposing crimes in Viet Nam from 1945 to 1967, it was a media sensation. When the *Washington Post* published the Afghanistan Papers in 2019, exposing the lies, deceits, mismanagement, waste, corruption, and fraud, there was hardly a whimper despite thousands of lives and costing over a trillion dollars. The Afghanistan Papers reveal that senior US officials failed to tell the truth since the wars beginning in 2001 while making rosy pronouncements they knew to be false and hid unmistakable evidence that the war was unwinnable. According to *Money Maven*, a network of economists and researchers, the wars since 9/11 have cost US taxpayers 6.4 trillion dollars. We can measure these forever wars in lost lives and money that society could have spent on the environment, infrastructure, education, social programs, and lower taxes.

FAILED ATTEMPTS

There are no quick fixes to our problems, and no amount of creditism will grow the economy in the long-run, but there have been attempts. Senator Frank Church chaired the Church Committee in the 1970s to investigate abuses by the Central Intelligence Agency, the National Security Agency, the Federal Bureau of Investigation, and the Internal Revenue Service. The Committee found that the President or Congress had little authority; the deep state made up their own rules and did horrible things like assassinating foreign leaders, overthrowing governments, creating secret alliances, and spying on US citizens. Congress passed the first Foreign Intelligence Surveillance Act in 1978, designed never to allow rogue behavior without Congressional approval and executive consent.

President Ronald Reagan established the Grace Commission in 1984. For two years, 160 corporate executives and community leaders led an army of 2,000 volunteers to root out government waste—volunteer contributors with zero cost to the government-funded search. The Commission made 2,478 recommendations over 21,000 pages to cut costs without eliminating essential services to make the federal government more efficient and accountable to the taxpayer.

Congress passed the Gramm-Rudman-Hollings Act in 1985 as a follow-up to the Grace Commission, otherwise known as the Balanced Budget and Emergency Deficit Control Act. This act mandated the government live within its income and provided for automatic spending cuts to take effect if the president and Congress failed to reach established spending targets. The act gave the U.S. comptroller general authority to order spending cuts when necessary to meet spending goals. When the courts declared the law unconstitutional, Congress passed a revised version of the bill in 1987. Instead of implementing needed reform and adhering to the law, Congress increased borrowing and spending.

President Obama formed the Simpson-Bowles Commission, co-chaired by Erskine Bowles and Alan Simpson, to find remedies for the credit crisis of 2010. The Commission outlined an ambitious package of spending cuts and tax increases and called for deep cuts in spending, a gradual rise in the federal gasoline tax, limiting popular tax breaks, and a child tax credit and the earned-income tax credit. It also called for an increase in the retirement age for Social Security, gave options for overhauling the tax system, cut Pentagon weapons programs, and reduced cost-of-living increases for all federal programs, including Social Security. Although more than 60 percent of Congress supported its recommendations, it never saw the light of day. The Twin Towers attack on 9-11 sealed our fate because it justified an aggressive foreign policy, including assassinations of foreign leaders, regime change wars, and unrestrained spending and debt.

WHAT A TANGLED WEB WE WEAVE

When countries trade, they struggle with bookkeeping. So, instead of exchanging money each day, a clearinghouse cancels debts among its members and then posts the debits and credits. If I owe you one thousand dollars and you owe me eight hundred dollars, it makes no sense for me to give you a thousand dollars, and then you give me eight hundred dollars. Instead, we clear the eight hundred dollars, and I owe you two hundred dollars. But instead of me giving you two hundred dollars, we enter this on a ledger because maybe tomorrow you will owe me. Since the 1970s, the Federal Reserve of New York has provided clearinghouse services.

The Society for Worldwide Interbank Financial Telecommunications (SWIFT) acts as an international clearinghouse by fast and (allegedly) secure international financial transfers. SWIFT transmits information using a standardized system of codes assigned to each bank. It does not hold funds, nor does it manage client accounts, but it is a system of tracking credits and debits amongst the world banks. Nearly 10,000 members send about 24 million messages on the network every day. America has expelled countries from SWIFT to sanction them for not supporting its policies. When the French bank BNP Paribas violated US sanction laws by trading with Iran, Sudan, and Cuba, a New York court fined the bank $9 billion, and the US threatened to exclude the bank. Paribus paid the fine because it depends on SWIFT for its international transactions.

Some countries have bilateral agreements using their currencies, the Chinese yuan, or gold to circumvent the SWIFT system. For example, Moscow and Tehran have turned away from the greenback in bilateral trade and are using the Russian ruble and Iranian rial for payments. Russia has also announced it is working towards replacing the dollar while conducting business with African nations instead of the Chinese yuan and European euro. Moscow has been dumping the US dollar from its international reserves, and it has increased gold and forex reserves. Forex stands for foreign exchange reserves, which are money or other assets held by a country's central bank to pay its liabilities.

Russia, China, India, Turkey, and Iran have divested themselves of American securities, increased their gold holdings, and ditched the dollar. India is not antagonistic toward America, but it draws closer to China and has joined the Shanghai Cooperation Organization picking up the slack caused by the US-China trade war. Turkey, a member of NATO, is moving closer to China, and it has dumped US securities while repatriating tons of gold from the Federal Reserve. It does not make much sense for countries to hold the debt of a country that threatens them. The Kremlin claims that the US has shot itself in the foot by placing sanctions against Russia by forcing it to offer higher returns to negate the risk factor. Investors seem to agree because Russian bonds are deemed more appealing than those of the US. Even Japan, a staunch ally of America, has been in talks with China to increase trade.

Mark Carney, governor of the Bank of England, gives speeches warning people of a dollar collapse and SWIFT's demise. Speaking in Jackson Hole, Wyoming, to a group of bankers, Carney postulated how a rise in technology disrupts the current financial system and suggests a decline in the dollar's dominance. He claims that the relatively high costs of domestic and cross-border electronic payments are encouraging innovation, with new entrants applying new technologies. The US has threatened to cut all Russian and Iranian banks, financial institutions, and government agencies from using SWIFT. People refer to this cut off as a nuclear option.

Consequently, Russia, China, and other countries wish to untangle themselves from dependence on the dollar and SWIFT.

An alternative to SWIFT is necessary before countries can replace the dollar. Two alternative systems are Instrument in Support of Trade Exchanges (INSTEX) and Russia's Transfer of Financial Messages (SPFS). INSTEX allows nations to trade with Iran without using dollars or running transactions through American banks. So far, Belgium, Denmark, Finland, the Netherlands, and Sweden have agreed to connect with INSTEX and normalize trade with Iran. Russia established Transfer of Financial Messages (SPFS) in 2014 to decrease the dependence on the dollar.

Getting rid of the greenback is no easy task. It took the US dollar nearly a century to unsettle the British pound that was the standard currency through the 19th and the first half of the 20th century. Iran, Malaysia, Turkey, and Qatar are using gold and barter for trade to shield themselves from future US punitive measures. Even the European Commission has plans to abandon the dollar in the energy sector, which would isolate America from most countries. Attendees at the World Economic Forum in Davos, Switzerland, discussed a central bank digital currency to replace the dollar. America's Achilles heel is rising interest rates and ditching the US dollar as the world's standard currency.

Events are splitting the United States, Japan, and Israel on one side and Russia, China, Germany, and Iran on the other side. Vladimir Putin has stated that Russia is moving towards independence from the dollar, not because he wants to undermine the dollar, but because he wants to insulate Russia from US sanctions. Russia favors a Eurasian perspective, cooperation between Europe and Asia, and seeks to partner with China and India. Because other nations distrust America, some are moving away from dependence on the once-mighty dollar.

MORALITY TRUMPS COMMON SENSE

Thomas Jefferson once said that *"America should have commerce with all nations and alliances with none. Money and not morality is the principle commerce of civilized nations."* But events took a turn when people began to place morality above commerce. In his book *The Rule of Nobody: Saving America from Dead Laws and Broken Government*, Philip K. Howard explains how detailed regulations have squashed creativity in America. Instead of general principles and common sense, society has come under the heavy yoke of rules instead of people. People pass on, but the rules stay behind.

The American Centrifuge Project in Ohio is the only operating facility utilizing advanced uranium enriched technology. Even though nuclear power is critical to protect national security and economic independence, Congress voted to dismantle the centrifuges to save the planet from nuclear energy. Because higher education has also taken the moral high ground, students educated in atomic power have fallen to near zero, so America will not have the expertise to replace its aging atomic facilities. William Scott Ritter Jr. is a former United Nations weapons inspector in Iraq from 1991 to 1998; he claims that America may never recover from the lack of expertise. Los Angeles, the largest city in California, has taken the moral high ground by proposing a gasoline car ban by 2030; the state's governor has issued an executive order banning gas-powered cars by 2035 in favor of electric vehicles. But California's strict climate policies are already causing electricity blackouts in the state, and the push for electric vehicles makes California more dependent on China for essential components for electric motors.

The European Union is also committing economic suicide by placing morality above commerce. For example, Dutch farmers put on a massive demonstration to protest stringent carbon and nitrogen emissions regulations that the Hague, the government of Holland, imposed on them. Even though Dutch farmers are known for their environmental conscientiousness, quality, and efficiency, the Hague buckled under pressure from the EU to meet the new emission standards.

Globalist France has taken the moral high ground by a devastating de-industrialization process where it has shipped manufacturing jobs to third-world countries. Simultaneously, cosmopolitan urban areas, such as Paris, have received a disproportionate infusion of financial capital leaving rural areas destitute and factory workers who live outside of Paris and other cities unemployed. To find jobs, workers have to commute to the cities—but they cannot live in the cities because it is too expensive. Workers cannot work where they live, and they cannot live where they work! Commuting can take as much as two hours each day. Then, in the name of morality, the French government imposed a fuel tax on the commuters to reduce carbon emissions. So, while the Yellow Vest Movement morphed into a massive rebellion against globalism, it started with a carbon tax.

The US has taken the moral high ground by legalizing corruption. When corporations hire lobbyists, we do not call it bribery. By calling it lobbying, we make the practice of influencing legislation in Congress morally acceptable. America has imposed sanctions and tariffs and weaponized the dollar while touting its morality as it accuses other countries of being ethically deficient. The reality is that America's character has declined. For example, the US's engineering culture has decayed—making money has superseded sound economic principles of investing. Russia and China support and reward their engineers for what they can produce, not by a rising stock price.

The sex and gender revolutionaries have the upper hand in public education and they have taken the moral high ground. For example, the Austin Independent School District has implemented a pornographic sex education policy and a pro-LGBTQ (Lesbian, Gay, Bi-sexual, Transgender, Queer) curriculum in grade school through high school. This radical program provides explicit instruction on gender identity and mandates support for the LGBTQ movement. Schools teach students how to obtain an abortion or obtain birth control pills without parental consent. Such policies fuel the fires of Christians and others who favor traditional values to push back against the LGBTQ movement. The American Medical Association, a professional organization of over 200,000 doctors, has passed a ruling that if a child comes home from school and claims he or she is of the opposite sex and the parents bring the child to a psychologist, the psychologist must support the child. This decision gives the child a veto over the parents and is an attack against the traditional family.

The federal government has transformed public education by making it a rule via Title One that any child who has special needs must have those needs met. A school system can best help these students in a self-contained classroom; however, to avoid government mandates and high expenses, public schools have reclassified needy students and have put them into less expensive regular classes. This practice has led to teacher burnout and a decline in the quality of public education.

CHAPTER 11

THE FUTURE

C hina became the first country to implement 5G technology throughout the country and now builds more 5G stations than rest of the world combined. The 5G network, which stands for "fifth generation," is a mobile telecommunications service that promises to be significantly faster than today's 4G technology. It takes four minutes to download a two-hour movie with 4G and only 3.6 seconds with 5G. Just like trains need tracks, 5G phones need a 5G network of towers. Investment in 5G lags behind China as American leaders engage in trade and currency wars, while China invests in its future. According to the *Globalist*, China's economy is more than three times greater than that of Germany and four and a half times larger than France or the United Kingdom.

Huawei is the world's largest telecom equipment and smartphones producer overtaking Samsung and Apple, with 29 percent of the global communications market and 70 percent of the Chinese market. It is poised to control more than half the 5G market even though it is on the US Entity List, which restricts its access to American technology. Huawei has released a smartphone with fully upgraded 5G technology, and its operating system does not rely on Google. Russia and China have teamed up with the company and installed the world's first 5G network in Moscow and Kronshtadt. Huawei now sells a folding smartphone without Google apps or the US made processor chips.

America has weaponized the dollar and militarized our relationship with friends and foes alike. But embargoes, sanctions, and military intervention will only lead to a decline. Once Google mobile services, including the Android operating system, dominated the mobile OS market. But because of US sanctions against Huawei and its customers, Huawei has replaced the Android system with its own Harmony mobile operating system. It has partnered with India's top 150 app developers to boost its offerings even more.

America has locked Huawei out of the American market and has ordered its allies to ban Huawei, without supplying proof of spying. Despite American threats, countries continue to do business with the company. Germany and the United Kingdom have refused to bow to Washington's demands stating that they will not exclude 5G providers just because they come from China. The stakes are high because the super-fast network will power any piece of sophisticated electronic equipment, and the US has no 5G provider to match Huawei's expertise. In fact, in the last 20 years, every American producer of telecommunication equipment is gone. Only Ericsson and Nokia are left to compete with Huawei while it has contracts to build a 5G network in Berlin, Hamburg, Munich, Cologne, and Frankfurt by the end of 2021. By 2022, 30 German cities with 16 million people will have Huawei's 5G network. Portugal and Switzerland have defied US warnings and has partnered with the company.

ZTE is another Chinese company that America sanctions. Alibaba's founder, Jack Ma, has spoken out against the trade war between China and the US, calling it the *stupidest thing in the world.* Alibaba is a Chinese multinational conglomerate specializing in e-commerce, retail, Internet, and technology and is the sixth-largest Internet company by revenue. This conflict is not a trade war as it is a techonomic war because China has plans to surpass the United States as the world's next techonomic superpower.

BELT and ROAD

The Belt and Road Initiative (BRI) is a trillion-dollar global vision to invest in developing countries' infrastructure. The belt refers to an overland transport link across China to Asia and Europe. The road refers to a network of maritime routes connecting China with the middle east, North Africa, Russia, and Europe. First introduced in 2013, the BRI will eventually link China with more than 100 countries. "China will actively promote international cooperation through the Belt and Road Initiative," President Xi Jinping said in 2017. *"In doing so, we hope to achieve policy, infrastructure, trade, financial and people-to-people connectivity and thus build a new platform for international cooperation to create new drivers of shared development."* Italy is the first EU country to join the initiative. In May of 2017, twenty-eight heads of state and delegates from 61 international organizations attended the Belt and Road Forum in Beijing. However, the US has threatened European countries with sanctions if they participate in the Belt and Road.

China has pledged $900 billion to build roads, railroads, ships, and sea routes to connect 64 countries in Asia and Europe and plans to build 60 airports. This trade route will cover over half the world's population and much of global GDP. For example, Gwadar's Pakistani town was a poor town of cinder block houses ringed by cliffs, deserts, and the Arabian Sea—it was at the forgotten edge of the earth—now it's a centerpiece of China's initiative.

EU countries will support the New Silk Road because the trend is for Europe to be more independent as events are splitting the world into two camps. There will be a deepening of differences between Europe and America, and it will become more apparent that the US is having less and less influence over Europe and the world. The more the US pressures Europe to cooperate with America's economic policies, the more it compels EU countries to choose between America and Eurasia.

The Belt and Road initiative and the completion of natural gas pipelines from Russia to Europe make Europe more dependent on Eurasia and less dependent on the US. In addition, Russia completed a railway and highway bridge over the Amur River in 2019. This bridge that connects Russia and China is 1.4 miles long and opened in 2020. The project aims to be an international corridor connecting China's northeastern railway networks with Russia's Siberian railway networks. Russia plans on exporting iron ore, coal, mineral fertilizers, lumber, and other goods to China because the bridge will shave off over 2,000 miles between the two countries. Russia is also committed to a massive infrastructure project by building a 1,243-mile road from the Belarus border in the north of Russia to Kazakhstan, which borders China in the south. Beijing plans to invest $114 billion in building its railways in 2020 to cover 98 percent of its countryside with delivery networks.

BIOMETRIC IDENTIFICATION

Utilizing the Freedom of Information Act (FOIA), John Greenewald Jr. has filed more than 8,000 FOIA requests. His web page https://www.theblackvault.com has more than 2,000,000 pages of declassified US Government documents ready to download on nearly any government secret you can imagine. For example, according to documents released under the Freedom of Information Act, the CIA has participated in mind control projects since the 1950s. The Central Intelligence Agency experimented on humans and animals to learn how to implant thoughts into brains. We are quickly approaching the day where there will be no place to hide, and privacy will be a thing of the past, even a criminal offense.

MasterCard and Microsoft have entered into a partnership to develop a universally recognizable digital identity, and LG has a phone where your hand is your identity. In a short while, we will produce phones with the ability to scan bodies biometrically. For example, China utilizes vein technology called "Deep Blue," which uses vein patterns to identify people. A digital ID contains a profile, such as buying habits, voting preferences, education, travel experiences, banking, etc.

A few years ago, parents were shocked when their son or daughter announced that they were gay or transgender—now, some young people want to exist as data. BBC and HBO jointly produce a mini-series called "Years and Years." At one point, the daughter explains that she is a transhumanist, and she wants to exist as data. Transhumanism is a cultural and intellectual movement that believes we can, and should, improve the human condition through the use of advanced technologies. An example of transhumanism is the Borg in the series Star Trek. The Borg are organisms with cybernetic components linked in a hive-mind called "the Collective." Facebook is developing a system in which you will be able to type out words and messages using only your brain. You will have to wear a device, but a computer chip implanted into your brain will allow you to interact with machines and other people mentally. Alvin Toffler predicted a future society in his 1970 book *Future Shock*, whereby people cannot adjust to the quickening pace of society due to technological change.

The Vatican has held a series of transhumanism conferences where globalists have met in the Vatican City to discuss the best path forward with humanity and technology in harmony. The keynote speakers of a recent meeting were Carlos Moreira and David Fergusson, who co-authored a book titled *The Transhuman Code: How to Program Your Future*. Another speaker was Fr. Philip Larrey, who authored a book titled *Artificial Humanity: An Essay on the Philosophy of Artificial Intelligence*. The conference's theme was a look into the transhuman future where humanity can thrive—balancing humans and machines. The Christian

Transhumanist Association has meetings each year in Nashville, Tennessee, at Lipscomb University. The world is rushing into a new existence, a new consciousness.

CRYPTOCURRENCIES

Cryptocurrencies are as revolutionary today as the internet was in 1994. The internet changed the way the world communicates, and cryptocurrencies change the way money works. Digital currencies are virtual, but not necessarily crypto. Cryptocurrencies, such as Bitcoin and Ethereum, have no central issuing or regulating authority but instead uses a peer to peer decentralized system to record transactions on a blockchain and manage the issuance of new units.

You can view the different cryptocurrencies in different rooms. For example, you can be in the Bitcoin room with other people using Bitcoin or be in the Ethereum (Ether) room with others using the same currency. The combined value of all Ether and Bitcoin is now worth more than the market value of PayPal and is approaching the size of Goldman Sachs. The value of these cryptocurrencies has no top because fiat currencies have no bottom. Ethereum was launched in 2015 by a 21-year-old college dropout, Vitalik Buterin, born in Russia and raised in Canada. He now lists his residence, jokingly, as Cathay Pacific Airlines because of his travel schedule. He is the world's youngest crypto billionaire.

Blockchain technology is a digital record of every transaction which programmers group into digital blocks. Any changes or additions to the Block must be verified by other participants on the network, making it almost impossible to alter the information. The blockchain is a public ledger that keeps track of every transaction since the system began, and all sales are shared and maintained on the network. The first Bitcoin transaction for a tangible good was a person who offered 10,000 Bitcoins to anyone who would buy him a pizza from Papa Johns. Africa leads other nations in Bitcoin; some Africans use it to purchase cars from Japan and Iran to avoid US sanctions.

Let's say you own a business, and you want to set a blockchain network to trace transactions. How do you do it? Dan Larimer will provide expertise. Through its open-source platform, Block.one will help you build a blockchain network. You can find more information about Block.one at https://block.one/. Larimer created the Steem cryptocurrency, which owners can exchange for other cryptocurrencies. Steemit is a social media platform where everyone gets paid for developing content. It leverages a digital point system (Steem) for digital rewards. Block.one has risen from nonexistence to a billion-dollar company in just two years.

Walmart currently uses the blockchain to track over one million items. It used to take Walmart a week to trace the origin of a piece of fruit—the blockchain network can find the same information in a few seconds. Corporate spending on blockchain software is in the billions of dollars a year, and the country of Dubai intends to make itself the first blockchain-powered government. Kingsland University, founded by Jason King, is the first accredited university teaching blockchain technology and educating and training blockchain developers. The university does not charge students tuition until they secure a job. Jason spends much of his time traveling the world, feeding the homeless, and teaching blockchain technology.

Cryptocurrencies will put a bullet hole through the heart of the central bankers and fiat currencies as they favor individual sovereignty; they go back to the era of honest money. The twenty-first century's new wars are ideological, media, and economic as nations are becoming ever more sophisticated and deploy cyber tools more aggressively. A Russian bank has issued a loan secured by cryptocurrency for the first time in history, and the government has passed a law recognizing the buying and selling of cryptocurrencies.

China is prepared to launch its digital currency, and the US Federal Reserve has partnered with MIT to develop a digital currency equivalent to cash. At some point, most countries will have their digital money, but these currencies are no better than traditional government-backed fiat currencies because they are not crypto. For a currency to be "crypto," it needs to be private, anonymous, and not controlled by a central authority.

Revolutionaries birthed cryptocurrencies out of a rebellion against the world's central bankers because the pier to pier system can replace fiat currencies. When the world's central banks partner with governments to issue digital currencies, the government will trace every transaction. Banks will then have complete control and will be able to block transactions if we dare to transgress against government policies or not support the official narrative. The government may even decide what we can and cannot purchase with our digital money. Of course, governments hate competition, and they will do what they can to limit access to cryptocurrencies, but we are too far down the crypto road to turn back now.

BITCOIN

In 2008, Bitcoin's inception took place by a White paper titled "Bitcoin - a peer to peer electronic cash system" by Satoshi Nakamoto, an unknown person. Fed up with the centralized and corrupt banking system, Nakamoto issued the first block of a maximum of 21 million in the blockchain that will eventually come into existence. The 30,000 lines are open-source, copyright-free, and available to everyone. People mine Bitcoins by solving computer codes to add transactions to the public blockchain resulting in a predictable fixed increase in the money supply. However, mining rewards decrease over time, putting a cap on the number of coins in existence. Investors deposit their Bitcoins in digital wallets at exchanges.

JPMorgan Chase Bank, the largest US bank by total assets, believes that Bitcoin is drawing investors away from gold because financial institutions view Bitcoin as an alternative to gold in terms of safety and return and displaces gold. Front running, the act of capitalizing on nonpublic knowledge by some investors, has also undermined the gold market. The biggest fund manager in the world, Blackrock, is divesting itself of gold and purchasing Bitcoin, according to cointelegraph.com. Rick Rieder, Blackrock's CIO of Fixed Income, told CNBC that *Bitcoin is here to stay.*" He stated that the currency would take the place of gold because it is more functional than gold. Citibank's director predicts that a Bitcoin unit will reach $318,000 by December 2021 as the dollar declines in value.

Cyber-attacks of hackers sending thousands of phantom transactions have disrupted exchanges. The most dramatic attack was on Mt. Gox, where Bitcoin fell to about $135 from $828.99 on Feb. 7, 2014, resulting in owners losing a lot of money. Mt. Gox was established in 2010 by Mark Karpeles and by 2014 was handling over 70 percent of Bitcoin transactions worldwide. Still, it had to file for bankruptcy after losing the coins of thousands of customers. TradeHill was the second-largest Bitcoin exchange. CEO Jared Kenna and cofounder Ryan Singer cited regulatory problems to close the firm's doors in 2012. The failure of Mt. Gox and TradeHill is not the end of Bitcoin because venture capitalists and Wall Street firms invest in Bitcoin's infrastructure—the age of cryptocurrencies is here to stay. Iceland spends more money mining Bitcoin at its Enigma facility than it spends on electricity for its houses. The official website at https://Bitcoin.com reads: "Digital money that's instant, private, and free from bank fees. Download our official wallet app and start using Bitcoin today."

The New York Stock Exchange (NYSE) lists a Bitcoin price index (NYXBT). NYXBT will represent the daily US dollar value of one Bitcoin at 4 pm (BST) daily. Selling digital coins online is a big business. A decentralized monetary system based on bits and bytes can be viable with enough support. Physical currencies represent a shared standard of value by keeping track of who owes whom—cryptocurrencies can do the same. A book on the subject is *The Age of Cryptocurrency: How Bitcoin and Digital Money are Challenging the Global Economic Order*, by Paul Vigna and Michael J. Casey, St. Martin's Press, 2015. In their book, the authors answer the question, "Why should anyone care about Bitcoin?"

According to the UK's *Telegraph* newspaper, the Winklevosses brothers are the first "Bitcoin billionaires." They purchased 100,000 units in 2013 when the price reached a high of $1,000 in November. Ethereum raised $12 million in just 10 minutes in April of 2017 and has produced more millionaires than any public company in history. Bitcoin became an asset class when Bloomberg terminal installed its first Bitcoin ticker. Now bankers can direct their multi-trillion-dollar pool of assets and point it toward destination Bitcoin. On November 19th, 2013, the currency moved more money than Western Union.

Bitcoin is poised to launch a revolution that could reinvent traditional financial and social structures while bringing billions of people into a new global economy. Cryptocurrencies hold the promise of a system without the middleman. No digital currency will replace the dollar soon, but the technology will become ever more popular. Switzerland's financial regulator has granted licenses to two blockchain companies, the first crypto banks. The companies will be able to issue, store, trade, and manage Bitcoins and Ethereum. The banks will also be able to convert fiat currencies into the two cryptocurrencies. In addition, Portugal's tax authority has announced that it will not tax gains on cryptocurrencies.

CRYPTO EXCHANGES

BitPay is a Bitcoin payment service provider in Atlanta, Georgia that provides Bitcoin and Bitcoin Cash payment processing services for merchants. Tether (USDT) is a cryptocurrency designed to mirror the value of the US dollar. As you can see, crypto exchanges explode in popularity as crypto exchanges allow owners of cryptocurrencies to trade with one another. We are experiencing a marriage between the crypto world and the traditional world as more and more people seek stability in this increasingly unstable world. The state of Wyoming is at the forefront of this crypto movement, with its special-purpose depository bank specializing in crypto transactions. Formally known as a Special Purpose Depository Institution (SPDI), a Speedy Bank will provide essential crypto services. And so we have a Special Purpose Depository Institution that gets created for full-fledged banks. The bank is still in the process of obtaining a bank charter from the United States authorities. Caitlin Long, who led the Wyoming Blockchain Task Force, says the primary purpose of SPDIs is to store private keys. A private key is simply a number, picked at random. Owners use a private key to create signatures to spend their Bitcoins.

Wyoming recognizes cryptocurrencies as legal property and gives people custody over digital assets. Thus, a pension fund that wants to invest in digital assets can now do so legally. Other states are considering their crypto banks, and even the chairman of the Federal Reserve is talking about the future of cryptocurrencies. In 2019, Congress passed the Bank Secrecy Act Reform Legislation, which attempts to modernize US banking laws to accommodate digital currencies. Innovation happens. Mexico, Argentina, Chile, Brazil, and Venezuela are adopting Bitcoin as legal tender and sponsor Bitcoin conferences. Can we take control of our money or continue to be under the authority of the world bankers?

GOVERNMENTS FIGHT BACK

Not everyone is on board with this new crypto world; for example, India has placed a total ban on private cryptocurrencies. The government is considering giving a 10-year prison sentence to anyone dealing with unregulated digital assets. In place of private cryptocurrencies, India plans to set up a "Digital Rupee" issued by its Reserve Bank as legal tender. Authorities fear that privately generated digital currencies "lack all the attributes of a currency," carry no "intrinsic value," and, therefore, can be detrimental to the economy. In addition, Indian authorities have stated that cryptocurrencies are inconsistent with essential functions of money, and consequently, they cannot replace fiat currencies.

CHAPTER 12

CONCLUSION

So far, the military-industrial complex, the neoconservatives, and the City of London has controlled the narrative and orchestrated events. But there is a growing backlash against the masters of the universe. Dr. Chuck Baldwin is a radio broadcaster, syndicated columnist, and pastor dedicated to preserving the historic principles of America. Following is a paraphrase from one of his weekly columns. The IRS has conquered our churches, COVID-19 has stolen our freedom, greed, and the lust for power has gripped our politicians. Godless education has captivated our children's minds, amoral movies and social media conquered our youth, and the mainline news will make you a slave to propaganda.

Archbishop Carlo Maria Vigano wrote a letter to President Trump dated June 6, 2020, warning him that the COVID-19 crises and the recurring riots are part of an eternal spiritual struggle between the forces of good and evil.

" ... On the other hand, there are those who serve themselves, who do not hold any moral principles, who want to demolish the family and the nation, exploit workers to make themselves unduly wealthy,

foment internal divisions and wars, and accumulate power and money."

END OF EMPIRE

Two aspects of the modern world support the American empire. First, the neoliberal economic policies have created a global casino economy in which the upper one percent control the house, and everyone else is the subject of predatory looting. Second, the empire utilizes a geopolitical operation, attacking any nation that does not submit. As the empire disintegrates, opposing forces have diminished our freedom and divided the country. Regime change, trade, and currency wars have weakened the nation, and the excessive debt contributes to a weak economy and a shrinking middle class. Empires in decay embrace an almost willful suicide, blinded by their hubris and unable to face the reality of their diminishing power. The United States has retreated into a fantasy world where unpleasant facts do not penetrate and where its leaders have been naive of the actual consequences of their actions. Empires thrive on the mystique made possible by past accomplishments; the mystique masks the plunder and exploitation of the kingdom—America is losing its mystique.

The expansion of the empire beyond its ability to sustain it makes the system vulnerable, especially during a depression. When an empire puts undue resources into building and maintaining the realm, when it spends more on the military and less on its citizens, the empire disintegrates. When an empire's overextension leads to decline, things unravel very quickly with worsening economic conditions. The decrease of law and order, the increase in unemployment, the collapse of the social welfare system, and people's inability to cope will lead to riots in the streets.

Washington has pulled out of the Cold War Era Intermediate-Range Nuclear Treaty (INF), blaming Moscow for failing to comply and raising fears of a new nuclear arms race. Since 1987 America and Russia have kept the lid on nuclear weapons—that agreement no longer exists. Could we be facing a new arms race between the world's superpowers? China was not a part of the 1987 agreement, but now that the deal is caput, we live in a more uncertain world. The treaty banned all short and medium-range missiles, both nuclear and nonnuclear land-based weapons. Both countries were allowed to inspect each other's installations. The latest abandoned agreement is the Open Skies Treaty, which allowed limited flights over each other's facilities. Only the New Start Treaty limiting long-range nuclear weapons exists between the US and Russia. When the world is facing an unprecedented economic crisis, the United States should be leading the international community, cooperating with allies, and avoiding actions that could further destabilize the global environment—the decision to withdraw from the Open Skies Treaty does the opposite.

The top one percent's growing assets are inversely related to the debts of the bottom 99 percent. When it is mathematically impossible to pay the debts off, either society can wipe out the obligations and grow again or leave the 99 percent in bondage and despair. Increasing taxes on the one percent is not the solution to the problem; only a debt forgiveness program and a new financial system will help because our current monetary system is debt-based. We must break the hold of the world bankers and establish a national or cryptocurrency economic system. Real democracy is not possible with a few billionaires controlling the purse strings. Money is like manure; you have to spread it around to be effective, which we are not doing. The authorities did not prosecute anyone in 2008 because the most prominent bankers were above the law.

When wealthy people engage themselves by inventions and innovations, when they build businesses, hire workers, and grow the economy, that kind of system is an industrial capitalistic economy. But this is not what we have today. Instead, what we have is a capitalistic finance economy—where the goal is to make money from money. The system secures money by real estate, stocks, bonds and not building a prosperous economy. When money is made by buying businesses to slice and dice to the highest bidder, instead of investing in research and development, capitalism does not work for the greater good.

There is a financial front running, and there is a political front running. The insiders know what the Federal Reserve and the government will do ahead of time, so they front-run to take advantage of the situation, and their wealth increases. The billionaire Warren Buffet has been privy to information, enabling him to make a fortune by front running the stock market. The question for Americans is, "do we want an oligarchy, or do we want a democratic republic?"

The global crisis is so dire that only a directed resource mobilization among the leading nations can turn things around. A collaborative effort of the United States, China, Russia, India, Japan, England, Germany, and others in forming a new credit system will be a step in the right direction and the establishment of a new world health and hospital system. We need to address the grossly uneven distribution of wealth. The typical worker must gain from increases in productivity for real incomes to increase, and we must save more and borrow less. Education should support personal finance courses instead of feel-good courses.

The pandemic and people's willingness to obey government mandates have led to unchecked government power and the suspension of our liberties. *V for Vendetta* is a movie where a group uses a virus to enslave the population and establishes a totalitarian society. The film demonstrates, *"People shouldn't be afraid of their government. Governments should be afraid of their people."* More than 120 former top military officers have signed a letter outlining threats to American democracy. They claim that we are in a conflict like no other time since our founding in 1776 between supporters of "socialism and Marxism" and supporters of "constitutional freedom and liberty."

Americans were motivated to fight for freedom in World War Two, and thousands of brave soldiers died on Normandy Beach. Still, today, few are willing to stand up to a tyrannical government bent on taking away our freedoms. We are losing the privilege of privacy, freedom of speech and the press, freedom of assembly, freedom to work, operate a small business, attend concerts, and even go to church without restrictions. When California closed churches but not strip clubs, two megachurches started their service with mock burlesque dance routines to circumvent the law. Freedom is not free, but we must fight for it. Just as World War One, and the Great Depression of the 1930s, birthed violent leaders like Hitler, Mao, Mussolini, Stalin, the virus, the economic collapse, and the Woke Movement can obliterate even the concept of freedom.

In Martin Niemöller (1892-1984) words, a critic of Adolph Hitler, *"First they came for the Jews and I did not speak out ... Then the Communists and I did not speak out ... Then they came for the trade unionists and I did not speak out ... Then they came for me and there was no one left to speak out for me."*

When Germany's highest court ruled in 2020 that the European Central Bank's constant bailouts of the biggest banks in Europe were illegal, recognizing the transfer of wealth from the people to the banks is not justified. World leaders must take steps to end the City of London's special privileges and replace it with people-serving policies put forward by Alexander Hamilton and

Lyndon LaRouche. Thus far, no court has interfered with the massive transfer of wealth from the middle class to the wealthy, especially in developing countries. We must break the neoconservatives' stranglehold, the Deep State, the military-industrial complex, and we must reform the banking system. It may take Gideon's army to defend our constitution, the republic, and the presidency. Only when an awake public asserts their God-given liberties to gain back their freedom will governments quit using excuses to seize power that does not belong to them. The answer to 1984 is still 1776.

ABOUT THE AUTHOR

I grew up in the golden age of rock'n'roll; the fifties was a decade when music changed from being parent-friendly to teenagers going wild over Elvis Presley, Chuck Berry, and Jerry Lee Lewis. I started college in 1963, the year the Beatles appeared on the Ed Sullivan Show. I remember lying in bed and listening to songs like "Let it Be," "Help," and "A Hard Day's Night."

Then there was that sobering moment sitting in the bleachers at Eastern Michigan University and hearing that Lee Harvey Oswald had assassinated John F. Kennedy. Looking back, I can see that events were taking us from traditions of baseball, apple pie, and family dinners together, to a world that has grown darker.

Moving from Michigan with my wife, Kay, I was hired to teach economics at New River Community College in Dublin Virginia, which I am still doing 45 years later. This book is the result of the painful process I had to fight through the propaganda, the disinformation, false teachings, half-truths, and groupthink. Knowledge is power, but the mainline news media lacks truth, and therefore the average person lacks power. My search led me to the alternative news media where I found well-informed, truth-seeking, patriotic people.

www.ingramcontent.com/pod-product-compliance
Lightning Source LLC
Chambersburg PA
CBHW060929040426
42445CB00011B/863